AUTOMATED WEALTH

The Ultimate Guide to Vending Success

by
Jack Donovan

Copyright 2024 Lars Meiertoberens. All rights reserved.

No part of this book may be reproduced in any form or by any electronic or mechanical means, including information storage and retrieval systems, without permission in writing from the author. The only exception is a reviewer who may quote brief excerpts in a review.

Although the author and publisher have made every effort to ensure that the information in this book was correct at the time of going to press, the author and publisher accept no liability to any party for any loss, damage or disruption caused by errors or omissions, whether such errors or omissions are due to negligence. accident or any other cause.

This publication is intended to provide accurate and reliable information with respect to the subject matter covered. It is sold on the understanding that the publisher does not provide professional services. If legal advice or other expert assistance is required, the services of a competent professional should be sought.

The fact that an organization or website is mentioned in this work as a citation and/or potential source of further information does not imply that the author or publisher endorses the information the organization or website provides or the recommendations it makes.

Please keep in mind that websites listed in this work may have changed or disappeared between the time this work was written and the time it was read.

Automated Wealth

The Ultimate Guide to Vending Success

Contents

Introduction 1

Chapter 1: Understanding the Vending Machine Business 6
    The Evolution of Vending Machines 6
    Why Vending Machines Are a Profitable Business 9

Chapter 2: Getting Started 14
    Setting Your Goals 14
    Creating a Business Plan 18

Chapter 3: choosing the right vending machines 21
    Types of Vending Machines 21
    Key Features to Look For 24

Chapter 4: Selecting Prime Locations 29
    High-Traffic Areas 29
    Negotiating Agreements with Property Owners 33

Chapter 5: Understanding Your Market 37
    Identifying Target Demographics 37
    Analyzing Competitors 41

Chapter 6: Building Your Brand 45
    Creating a Memorable Brand Name 45
    Designing Logos and Branding Materials 48

Chapter 7: Sourcing Products 53
    Finding Reliable Suppliers 53
    Choosing the Right Product Mix 57

Chapter 8: Pricing Strategies 61
   Setting Profitable Prices 61
   Understanding Market Rates 64

Chapter 9: Machine Maintenance and Troubleshooting 68
   Routine Maintenance Guidelines 68
   Common Problems and Solutions 72

Chapter 10: Marketing Your Vending Business 77
   Utilizing Social Media 77
   Traditional Marketing Methods 81

Chapter 11: Legal Considerations 84
   Licensing and Permits 84
   Understanding Zoning Laws 87

Chapter 12: Financial Management 92
   Setting Up Your Accounting System 92
   Managing Cash Flow 95

Chapter 13: Operations and Inventory Management 100
   Tracking Inventory 100
   Restocking Efficiently 103

Chapter 14: Customer Service and Relations 107
   Handling Customer Complaints 107
   Building Customer Loyalty 110

Chapter 15: Technology and Innovations 114
   Utilizing Vending Software 114
   Integrating Cashless Payment Systems 118

Chapter 16: Automating Your Business 122
   Leveraging Automation Tools 122
   Reducing Manual Labor 126

Chapter 17: Expanding Your Business 130
   Scaling Strategies 130

  Considering Franchising 134

Chapter 18: Evaluating Your Success 139
  Key Performance Indicators 139
  Conducting Regular Reviews 143

Chapter 19: Case Studies of Success 147
  Interviews with Successful Vending Entrepreneurs 147
  Lessons Learned 150

Chapter 20: Industry Trends and Future Outlook 155
  Emerging Trends in Vending 155
  Preparing for the Future 158

Chapter 21: Dealing with Competition 162
  Competitive Pricing Strategies 162
  Differentiation Tactics 166

Chapter 22: Managing Risks and Challenges 169
  Identifying Potential Risks 169
  Mitigation Strategies 172

Chapter 23: Sustainability and Eco-Friendly Practices 176
  Green Vending Solutions 176
  Benefits of Sustainability 179

Chapter 24:0 Networking and Professional Development 183
  Joining Industry Associations 183
  Attending Conferences and Workshops 186

Chapter 25: Exit Strategies and Succession Planning 189
  Planning Your Exit 189
  Selling Your Business 192

Conclusion 196

Appendix A: Appendix 199

Introduction

Starting a vending machine business may sound like a simple venture, but it's loaded with hidden opportunities and potential pitfalls. Whether you're an aspiring entrepreneur or an existing business owner looking to diversify your income streams, this book is designed to guide you through everything you need to know about launching, managing, and expanding a profitable vending machine business.

The allure of passive income, where money flows in with minimal ongoing effort, is undeniably strong. For many, the vending machine business represents a perfect blend of low startup costs and high scalability. Yet, it isn't just about placing machines in random locations and hoping for the best. The vending industry has its own intricacies, requiring strategic planning, in-depth market analysis, and effective management skills.

First, let's admit it: vending machines are a part of our everyday lives, and they have been for quite some time. From grabbing a cold soda on a hot day to picking up a quick snack between meetings, these conveniences cater to our fast-paced lifestyles. The key lies in turning this convenience into a profitable business model. Through careful planning and execution, you can create a steady stream of revenue that grows over time.

This book is not just a manual; it's a roadmap. We start from the very basics, diving into the evolution of vending machines and why this industry remains profitable. Understanding the history and economics of vending machines will give you a solid foundation on which to build your business. You'll gain insights into how this industry evolved and the latest trends shaping its future.

Next, we'll dig into the essential steps to get your business off the ground. Setting clear, achievable goals and crafting a comprehensive business plan are crucial first steps. A well-thought-out plan serves as your North Star, guiding your decisions and making it easier to secure financing and attract partners. A clear roadmap will keep you focused and help you monitor your progress.

Choosing the right vending machines and selecting prime locations are paramount. Your research doesn't end here; it's just getting started. Different types of vending machines offer various features and functionalities, each suited to different markets and customer needs. In this guide, we'll explore these types and highlight key features to look for when making your selection.

Location is a critical factor in your vending machine business's success. Knowing where to place your machines for maximum visibility and foot traffic can make or break your venture. You'll learn the art of scouting high-traffic areas and negotiating agreements with property owners, giving you a competitive edge in securing prime spots.

The next step is understanding your market. Identifying your target demographics and analyzing your competitors are not tasks to be taken lightly. Understanding who your customers are and what they want ensures that your machines are stocked with the right products, leading to higher satisfaction and repeat business. Competitive analysis will also give you insights into what works and what doesn't, helping you refine your strategies.

A memorable brand name and strong branding materials can set you apart from the competition. Your brand is more than just a logo; it represents the values and quality you bring to the table. We'll walk through the process of creating an impactful brand that resonates with your target audience.

Of course, any vending machine is only as good as the products it offers. That's why sourcing quality products and developing a smart product mix is so crucial. Partnering with reliable suppliers ensures you always have the inventory you need to keep your machines stocked and customers satisfied. We'll guide you through choosing suppliers and crafting a product mix that maximizes your revenue.

As with any business, pricing strategies can be complex. Setting profitable prices while staying competitive requires a nuanced understanding of market rates and consumer behavior. You'll gain insights into how to price your products effectively without driving customers away or sacrificing profits.

Routine maintenance and the occasional troubleshooting are inevitable in this business. Regular maintenance ensures that your machines operate smoothly, reducing downtime and costly repairs. We'll provide guidelines for maintaining your machines and solutions for common problems that might arise.

Marketing your vending machine business goes beyond filling your machines with popular items. Utilizing both social media and traditional marketing methods can boost your visibility and attract more customers. We'll explore different marketing channels and strategies to help you build a loyal customer base.

Legal considerations are another crucial area to cover. From securing the necessary licenses and permits to understanding zoning laws, compliance isn't optional—it's essential. Legal issues can derail your business before it even starts, so we'll demystify the regulatory landscape.

Financial management is the backbone of any successful business. Setting up an accounting system and managing cash flow efficiently is fundamental. You'll learn how to track your income and expenses, allocate funds wisely, and prepare for taxes.

The day-to-day operations of running a vending machine business require effective inventory and restocking management. Keeping track of inventory levels and knowing when to restock will keep your machines running smoothly and profitably. Efficient operations lead to better customer satisfaction and increased revenue.

Excellent customer service and relations are often underestimated in vending, but they're vital. Handling complaints and building customer loyalty can create repeat business and positive word-of-mouth. We'll share tips on maintaining high customer satisfaction.

Technology and innovations play an increasingly crucial role in modern vending businesses. From vending software to cashless payment systems, leveraging technology can streamline operations and enhance customer experience. This guide will cover how to integrate these tech tools effectively.

As you grow more comfortable managing your business, you'll find ways to automate various aspects of operations. Reducing manual labor through automation tools not only saves time but also improves efficiency, giving you the freedom to focus on growth strategies.

Expanding your business is a natural next step once you've established a successful model. We'll discuss various scaling strategies, including potential franchising opportunities, to help you take your vending business to the next level.

Success doesn't happen overnight. Evaluating your progress through key performance indicators (KPIs) and conducting regular reviews helps you stay on track and make necessary adjustments. Continuous evaluation ensures long-term success and growth.

Learning from others who have walked the same path is invaluable. That's why we include case studies and interviews with successful vending entrepreneurs. Their experiences provide practical insights and lessons you can apply to your own journey.

Finally, keeping an eye on industry trends and future outlooks can position you ahead of the competition. Staying updated on emerging trends can help you adapt and innovate, ensuring that your business thrives in the long run.

The path to a successful vending machine business is filled with both challenges and rewards. By navigating each step strategically, you can turn your vision into a reality. Let's embark on this journey together, transforming aspiration into achievement, one vending machine at a time.

Chapter 1: Understanding the Vending Machine Business

Diving into the vending machine business is like stepping into a world of remarkable potential and timeless appeal. Our world has changed dramatically over the past century, yet vending machines have persisted and evolved, adapting to new consumer behaviors and technological advancements. What makes this business model so compelling for aspiring entrepreneurs and seasoned business owners alike? It's relatively low maintenance, requires minimal oversight, and offers a steady revenue stream—all while you enjoy the freedom that comes with passive income. Understanding the intricacies of this industry—how it has transformed over time and why it remains profitable today—sets the foundation for building a successful venture. By grasping the history and monetary allure of vending machines, you position yourself to make informed decisions that propel your business forward.

The Evolution of Vending Machines

The vending machine business, with its promise of passive income and low overhead, isn't a recent phenomenon. It has evolved dramatically over the decades, tracing its origins back to ancient times. The first vending machines date back to the 1st century AD in Egypt, where a temple engineer, Heron of Alexandria, invented a device that dispensed holy water when a coin was inserted. Fast forward many centuries, and modern vending machines began to appear in the early 1880s in London, dispensing postcards.

It wasn't until the early 20th century that vending machines began to offer a variety of goods more aligned with what we see today. In the 1920s, the U.S. saw the introduction of the first automated machines capable of selling soda, confectionery, and cigarettes. These machines were simple, accepting only one type of coin and dispensing one product. The innovation was revolutionary for its time, offering convenience and round-the-clock service that traditional retail couldn't match.

The post-World War II era was a golden age for the vending machine industry. Various factors contributed to this boom, including increased consumer spending, technological advancements, and a growing fascination with automation. Machines started to accept multiple coin denominations and even dispense change, making them more user-friendly. The 1950s and 1960s saw machines vending everything from coffee to hot food, paving the way for the versatility that characterizes today's vending machines.

By the 1970s and 1980s, vending machines began incorporating more sophisticated technology such as electronic payment systems. This period also saw the rise of specialized vending machines providing products like fresh sandwiches, newspapers, and even disposable cameras. The adaptability of vending machines became their biggest selling point, attracting both consumers and entrepreneurs alike.

Entering the late 20th century, the vending machine business started to globalize. Machines popped up in airports and train stations worldwide, catering to an increasingly mobile population. In Japan, vending machines became especially pervasive, selling not just food and drinks but a gamut of products including clothing and electronics. The Japanese market is a unique case study in the vending machine business, representing how a culture can embrace automated retail to an extraordinary extent.

In the 21st century, the pace of technological advancement accelerated, transforming vending machines into high-tech retail points. The advent of the internet brought about connected vending machines, enabling real-time inventory tracking, remote management, and dynamic pricing models. Machines started accepting cashless payments through credit cards and mobile wallets, aligning with consumer preferences for convenience and speed.

Recent years have seen even more innovations with the integration of AI and machine learning. Modern vending machines can now offer personalized recommendations based on purchasing habits. Some even use facial recognition technology to provide customized experiences. These advancements are not only enhancing user engagement but also optimizing inventory and improving operational efficiency.

The evolution of vending machines didn't stop at technological improvements. Social trends sparked new niches, such as healthy vending machines offering organic and low-calorie snacks. Sustainability also became a focus, with eco-friendly machines that use energy-efficient systems and biodegradable packaging. Entrepreneurs entering the vending business today have a wealth of opportunities to differentiate their offerings and tap into these emerging trends.

The COVID-19 pandemic acted as a catalyst for further innovations in the vending machine sector. As contactless interactions became paramount, the vending industry responded swiftly. Machines equipped with hand sanitizer dispensers, UV disinfection lights, and remote app-controlled features gained popularity. Additionally, there was a rise in automated kiosks dispensing PPE kits and food items, addressing immediate consumer needs during the crisis.

Looking globally, countries like China are rapidly adopting advanced vending solutions, integrating them into smart city initiatives. These machines are becoming more than just retail points; they serve as data collection hubs, gathering insights on consumer habits and preferences, which can be used to tailor services and products more precisely. This level of integration signifies a new era where vending machines play a more dynamic role in urban ecosystems.

As we move further into the 21st century, the future of vending machines looks promising and exciting. The blending of artificial intelligence, IoT, and sustainable practices will continue to shape the evolution of vending machines. Aspiring entrepreneurs have a unique opportunity to leverage these advancements, creating businesses that are not just profitable but also forward-thinking and resilient.

In essence, the vending machine industry has journeyed from dispensing rudimentary holy water in ancient temples to offering sophisticated, tech-driven retail solutions today. Understanding this evolution helps entrepreneurs appreciate the rich history and dynamic nature of this business, providing context for making informed decisions and embracing future innovations. Each step in this century-spanning evolution has brought new challenges and opportunities, setting the stage for yet another chapter in the fascinating story of vending machines.

With this historical perspective, you're now well-prepared to delve deeper into why vending machines are a profitable business in the next section. Let the lessons from the past guide your steps as you embark on this entrepreneurial journey, armed with the insights and knowledge to make your vending machine venture a thriving success.

Why Vending Machines Are a Profitable Business

The vending machine business has blossomed into a highly profitable venture, appealing to both aspiring entrepreneurs and seasoned business owners. Unlike many traditional businesses, the initial cost of entry for vending machines is relatively low, allowing you to start small and scale up as you generate revenue. The financial model is straightforward: a one-time investment in machines, minor recurring expenses, and a continuous stream of passive income. But the simplicity doesn't undermine its profitability; instead, it amplifies it by reducing overhead and maximizing returns.

One of the most compelling reasons vending machines are profitable is their versatility in location. High-traffic areas like office buildings, schools, hospitals, and shopping malls are gold mines for vending machine operators. The consistent foot traffic translates to frequent sales, enabling a steady cash flow that is often more reliable than other forms of retail. Plus, you have the flexibility to place machines in a variety of settings, each one tailored to the preferences and needs of the local demographic. The adaptability of vending machines opens up a world of possibilities for income generation.

Operating a vending machine business requires minimal hands-on involvement, offering a unique blend of automation and scalability. Machines operate around the clock, 24/7, ensuring sales are made even when you're not there. This is a stark contrast to traditional brick-and-mortar establishments that have restricted operating hours and require staffing. The automation allows you to manage multiple machines across different locations with minimal human intervention, multiplying your revenue-generating assets.

Product diversity is another factor contributing to the profitability of vending machines. Today's vending machines go beyond soda and snacks; they can dispense anything from healthy foods and beverages to tech gadgets and personal care items. By diversifying the product offerings, you can cater to a wide array of consumer preferences and even tap into niche markets. This diversification increases the likelihood of capturing repeat customers and boosting sales even further.

Low operational costs are a hallmark of the vending machine business. Aside from the initial investment in purchasing the machines, your primary expenses will be restocking products and routine maintenance. Unlike other businesses that may require paying for utilities, rent, and extensive staff, vending machines essentially eliminate many of those overhead costs. Some property owners might charge a small fee or a commission on sales for the placement of the machines, but these expenses are generally minimal compared to the potential profits.

Moreover, technological advancements have made vending machines smarter and more efficient. Modern vending machines come equipped with sophisticated software that monitors stock levels, sales data, and even mechanical issues in real-time. This enables you to anticipate when a machine needs restocking or maintenance, reducing downtime and keeping your operation running smoothly. Cashless payment options, such as credit card readers and mobile payment systems, have also broadened the customer base, making it easier for people to make purchases without the need for cash.

From a financial perspective, the return on investment (ROI) for vending machines is quite attractive. The capital required to purchase and install a vending machine can be recouped relatively quickly, often within a few months, depending on the location and product mix. Once you break even, the profit margins can be substantial, leading to a continuous stream of income. This quick ROI allows you to reinvest in additional machines or upgrade existing ones, facilitating growth and expansion of your vending machine empire.

The repetitive nature of the business also provides a predictable income stream. Unlike seasonal businesses that fluctuate in sales throughout the year, vending machines generally maintain a consistent level of sales. This predictability allows for better financial planning and forecasting, which is essential for long-term business stability and growth. It's a less volatile market compared to other forms of retail, providing a safer investment for those looking to diversify their income streams.

In addition, there's the psychological advantage of impulse purchases. Vending machines leverage the consumer habit of making quick, unplanned purchases. Whether it's the convenience of grabbing a snack during a work break or a bottle of water on a hot day, these small, impulsive buys add up quickly, significantly contributing to the overall profitability. The convenience factor shouldn't be underestimated, as it plays a crucial role in driving sales and profits.

Apart from the financial advantages, running a vending machine business allows you to cultivate valuable business skills and acumen. Managing inventory, negotiating with suppliers, selecting profitable locations, and analyzing sales data are all integral parts of the business. These skills are not only essential for running a successful vending machine business but are also transferable to other entrepreneurial ventures. It's an excellent way for novice entrepreneurs to get hands-on experience in managing a business without the overwhelming complexities of larger operations.

The vending machine industry is resilient, adapting well to various economic climates. In times of economic downturn, people often seek convenience and affordability, both of which vending machines provide. Conversely, during prosperous times, consumers might indulge more frequently in premium offerings from vending machines, such as high-end snacks or specialty beverages. This resilience insulates the business, making it a stable venture in both good and challenging economic conditions.

Lastly, the vending machine business offers opportunities for social impact and community engagement. Modern entrepreneurs are increasingly socially conscious, and vending machines can be tailored to promote healthier lifestyles or support local businesses by offering locally sourced products. Such initiatives not only boost your business reputation but also resonate with a growing segment of consumers who prioritize ethical and sustainable practices.

In conclusion, vending machines represent a golden opportunity for entrepreneurs seeking a profitable and low-maintenance business. Their ability to generate passive income, combined with low operating costs and high versatility, make them an attractive investment. The industry's adaptability to technological advancements and varying economic climates further solidifies its profitability. With strategic planning and execution, a vending machine business can provide a robust return on investment and an invaluable platform for entrepreneurial growth.

Chapter 2: Getting Started

As you embark on your journey into the vending machine business, the first crucial step is laying a solid foundation. This means understanding your personal and financial goals, followed by crafting a meticulous business plan. Whether you're an aspiring entrepreneur or an established business owner, pinpointing your objectives will guide your decisions and strategies. Think about why you're venturing into this field—perhaps it's to create a steady stream of passive income or to diversify your investment portfolio. Once your goals are clear, it's time to draft a business plan that covers everything from initial costs to operational strategies. This plan will be your roadmap, helping you stay on course and make informed financial and strategic decisions. Remember, a well-thought-out business plan is not just a formality; it's a blueprint for success, offering clarity and direction as you navigate the intricacies of the vending machine market.

Setting Your Goals

Before diving headfirst into the vending machine business, it's crucial to set clear and actionable goals. These goals not only keep you focused but also serve as a roadmap to gauge your progress over time. For many aspiring entrepreneurs and existing business owners, this initial step can make the difference between success and stagnation. So let's delve into how you can define your objectives effectively.

When it comes to goal-setting, specificity is paramount. Generic goals like "I want to be successful" are too vague. Instead, aim for something measurable and specific, such as "I want to earn $5000 per month in passive income within the first year." The more detailed your goals, the easier it will be to devise a plan to reach them. Break down your long-term goals into smaller milestones—monthly, quarterly, and yearly objectives can keep you motivated and on track.

Consider both your financial and personal aspirations. Think about how much you want to earn and how this income will impact your life. Do you want to replace a current job, supplement your current income, or build a scalable business that you can eventually sell? These considerations should guide your overarching strategy. For example, if your aim is to build a scalable business, your goals might include expanding the number of vending machines or entering new markets.

Time-bound goals are another crucial aspect. Setting deadlines for each objective gives you a sense of urgency and helps prioritize tasks. Without a timeline, your goals can become mere wishes. However, avoid overly ambitious deadlines that are impossible to meet, as this can lead to disappointment and burnout. Instead, balance ambition with realism by considering your initial capital, time commitment, and market research.

Having identified your financial targets and timelines, it's equally important to determine operational goals. These might include acquiring a certain number of machines, securing prime locations, or establishing relationships with product suppliers. Additionally, think about customer satisfaction and brand recognition. How will you measure success in these areas? Could you set targets related to customer feedback or social media engagement?

You'll also want to consider educational goals. Knowledge is power in the vending machine business. Whether it's learning about the latest technology or understanding market trends, setting goals for ongoing learning can significantly empower your business. Aim to read industry reports, attend trade shows, or even take a course on business management. These educational goals ensure you're not just reacting to changes in the market but anticipating them.

One of the most overlooked aspects of goal-setting is adaptability. The business landscape is always shifting, and your goals should have the flexibility to adapt to unforeseen circumstances. Building contingency plans and setting review periods to reassess your goals can help you stay resilient. For instance, if a new competitor enters the market or a global pandemic strikes, your ability to pivot quickly can set you apart from less prepared businesses.

Accountability plays a critical role in meeting your goals. Whether it's a mentor, business partner, or a close-knit entrepreneurial community, having someone to hold you accountable can be instrumental. Regular check-ins, progress reports, or even a simple conversation can help keep you motivated and on track. This network can also be a source of invaluable advice and encouragement, particularly when you hit inevitable roadblocks.

Let's not forget the importance of aligning your business goals with your personal values and lifestyle. Are you aiming for a business that allows you more freedom and flexibility, or are you ready to put in long hours to achieve rapid growth? Understanding your personal priorities can help you create a business model that's not just profitable but also sustainable in the long run. If business growth compromises your quality of life, you might need to recalibrate your goals.

Financial forecasting is another cornerstone of goal-setting. By projecting your revenue, expenses, and profits, you can set realistic financial goals. Calculate the break-even point—the moment when your vending business covers its costs and starts making a profit. Knowing this milestone and how long it will take to get there is crucial for long-term planning. Tools like cash flow statements, income statements, and balance sheets can help provide a clear financial picture.

Seek to establish a balanced scorecard. This strategic planning and management system can provide a holistic view of your business performance. It incorporates financial objectives with customer, process, and learning goals, giving you a comprehensive framework for success. With a balanced scorecard, you can track different facets of your business and make informed decisions that align with your long-term vision.

Defining your competitive edge is another often overlooked goal. In a market filled with vending machines, what will set yours apart? Consider goals related to unique selling propositions (USPs), such as offering healthier options, leveraging eco-friendly practices, or using advanced technology for a superior customer experience. By identifying what makes you unique, you can carve out a niche market that's eager for what you have to offer.

Don't underestimate the power of visualization in goal-setting. Business coaches and successful entrepreneurs alike often recommend visualizing your success. Whether it's through vision boards, affirmations, or regular meditative practice, seeing your goals in a tangible form can help keep you motivated and focused. Visualization bridges the gap between where you are and where you want to be.

Finally, remember that goal-setting is not a one-time activity. It's an ongoing process that requires regular review and adjustment. Make it a habit to revisit your goals periodically. Assess what's working, what's not, and why. Being proactive about refinements ensures that you're always moving in the right direction, even if the path changes form.

By approaching goal-setting with diligence and strategic thinking, you lay a solid foundation for your vending machine business. When your goals are clear, actionable, and aligned with your broader vision, you give yourself the best chance for sustained growth and success. So take the time now to chart your course—it will pay dividends in the long run.

Creating a Business Plan

At the heart of every successful business lies a well-thought-out plan. As you embark on your journey in the vending machine industry, it's crucial to create a comprehensive business plan that will act as your roadmap. This document will not only provide direction but also serve as a tool to attract potential investors and partners. A solid business plan can make the difference between a thriving venture and a failed attempt.

Your business plan should start with an executive summary. This is essentially a snapshot of your business, highlighting your objectives, the problem your vending machines will solve, and the unique selling proposition (USP) that sets you apart from competitors. Keep this section concise yet compelling—think of it as the "elevator pitch" of your business.

Next, move on to the company description. This section should provide more detail about your business, including the mission statement, values, and the specific niches you plan to target. Are you focusing on healthy snack options? Or perhaps tech gadgets? Clearly articulate what you're aiming to achieve.

Market research is another vital component. Analyzing the market helps you understand the landscape, identify opportunities, and anticipate challenges. Dive deep into demographic data, consumer behavior, and existing competition. This research will not only inform your strategies but also demonstrate to stakeholders that you've done your homework.

Incorporate a section that outlines your business structure and management. Who are the key players in your venture, and what experience do they bring to the table? Whether it's just you starting out or a small team, detailing the roles and responsibilities helps clarify the operational dynamics of your business.

Financial projections are crucial for any business plan. These should include income statements, cash flow projections, and balance sheets for at least the first three to five years. Make realistic assumptions and be prepared to justify them. Cash flow is particularly critical in the vending machine business, as it directly impacts your ability to restock and maintain machines.

Your marketing and sales strategy is where you'll outline how you plan to attract and retain customers. Will you use social media to generate buzz? Do you plan on partnering with local businesses for placement? Describe your advertising tactics, promotions, and customer engagement methods. Tailor your strategies to the market research you've conducted.

Discuss your operations plan in detail. This includes the logistics of stocking machines, maintenance schedules, and how you'll handle any issues that arise. Efficiency in operations can drastically reduce costs and increase profitability, so leave no stone unturned here.

Don't forget about the legal aspects. Outline any licenses or permits you need, as well as your plan to comply with local regulations. Understanding zoning laws and securing the necessary documentation is key to avoiding legal pitfalls down the line.

Risk management should also be addressed. Identify potential obstacles that could impact your business and propose mitigation strategies. Whether it's economic downturns, supply chain disruptions, or machine malfunctions, having a plan to tackle these issues will prepare you for the unexpected.

Lastly, include an appendix with any additional information such as resumes, product photos, or detailed market studies. This will provide readers with a fuller picture of your business without cluttering the main sections.

Remember, a business plan is a living document. It should evolve as your business grows and the market changes. Regularly review and update it to reflect new goals, market conditions, and strategies. With a well-prepared business plan, you're setting the foundation for a successful and profitable vending machine enterprise.

Chapter 3: Choosing the Right Vending Machines

Choosing the right vending machines is a critical step in building your vending machine business. The type of vending machines you invest in will directly influence your product offerings, maintenance schedules, and overall profitability. Whether you go for snack machines, beverage dispensers, combo units, or specialized machines for niche markets, each has its own set of advantages and considerations. To make an informed decision, you'll need to consider the specific needs of your target market, the locations you're aiming to place your machines in, and the latest trends in vending technology. Modern vending machines with touchscreens, cashless payment systems, and advanced inventory management software can offer significant benefits, but they also come with higher upfront costs. Balancing innovation with cost- effectiveness, and ensuring that the machines you choose meet the demands of your customers, will set the foundation for a successful and thriving vending machine operation.

Types of Vending Machines

Choosing the right vending machines can make or break your vending machine business. It's critical to understand the various types available, what they offer, and how they align with your business goals. Broadly speaking, vending machines can be categorized based on what they dispense: food and drink, hygiene products, books and electronics, and even specialized gourmet items. Each type caters to different customer needs and scenarios, allowing you to place machines strategically to maximize profitability.

First, let's talk about the classic and ever-popular food and drink vending machines. These often come to mind when people think of vending machines. They typically dispense snacks, beverages, or a combination of both. Snack vending machines usually carry an array of chips, candy bars, and other packaged goodies, while beverage vending machines are loaded with sodas, water, and sometimes coffee options. Combo machines offer a mix of both, making them a versatile option, especially in locations with limited space. These machines are ideal for break rooms, schools, hospitals, and transportation hubs where people seek quick refueling options.

A sub-category worth mentioning within food and drink machines is the refrigerated and frozen vending machines. These units can keep perishable items like sandwiches, salads, or even ice cream at the perfect temperature. They're a fantastic choice for locations that demand healthier or more substantial food options, like workplaces that promote wellness or fitness centers. Although these machines require more maintenance—such as regular temperature checks and timely restocking—the higher revenue potential can be worth the effort.

Another category that's growing in popularity is the hygiene and personal care vending machines. These machines offer items like toothbrushes, skincare products, and even feminine hygiene products. You might have seen them in airports, gyms, and hotels. The convenience they provide makes them a hit among travelers and individuals always on the go. In the age of heightened health awareness, these machines can offer hand sanitizers, face masks, and other hygiene essentials, making them a timely addition in public spaces.

Books, media, and electronics vending machines are also carving out a niche. Machines that dispense books or multimedia items like

DVDs (yes, they still exist!) are often found in airports and train stations, catering to travelers needing entertainment for long journeys. Electronic vending machines, on the other hand, have gained traction in the last decade. Imagine needing a charger for your phone or a pair of headphones while waiting for a flight. These machines can provide a solution instantly, making them invaluable in high-traffic, high-stress environments like airports and major transit stations.

Then, there are the highly specialized vending machines. For example, some machines dispense gourmet items such as fresh cupcakes, premium cuts of meat, or even seafood. They cater to a niche market but can bring in significant revenue, especially if placed in affluent areas or food-centric locales. Additionally, tech-savvy entrepreneurs are exploring options like cannabis vending machines in regions where it's legal or machines that dispense CBD products. These highly specialized machines require a deeper understanding of regulations and a more targeted marketing strategy, but they offer a unique selling proposition that can set your business apart.

The emergence of eco-friendly vending machines is also a trend worth noting. These machines focus on minimizing environmental impact by offering biodegradable or recyclable packaging and energy-efficient operation. Some even allow customers to refill their own containers, promoting a zero-waste lifestyle. Installing such machines can be a strong statement of your brand's commitment to sustainability and can appeal to a growing base of environmentally conscious consumers.

Operational features are another critical dimension to consider when choosing your vending machines. Machines vary in their payment systems—some only accept cash, while more modern models offer card payments, mobile payments, and even cryptocurrency options. The right choice here will depend on your target market's preferences.

Younger, tech-savvy customers might prefer machines equipped with the latest cashless payment technologies.

Furthermore, vending machines can be equipped with telemetry systems that provide real-time data on sales, inventory levels, and even maintenance needs. These "smart" machines can help streamline operations and reduce downtime, boosting your profitability. If you're planning to manage a large fleet of machines, investing in smart technology can offer significant advantages in operational efficiency and customer satisfaction.

Understanding these different types of vending machines will enable you to make more informed decisions as you build your vending machine business. By aligning the machine type with the specific needs and behaviors of your target market, you'll be better positioned to generate a steady stream of passive income. And remember, the landscape is always evolving. New types of vending machines and innovative features continue to emerge, offering fresh opportunities for those willing to seize them.

In summary, whether you're aiming to cater to snack-craving office workers, travelers in need of a quick charge, or eco-conscious consumers, there's a vending machine type that fits the bill. Carefully consider your target market and the locations you aim to serve, and choose machines that not only meet their needs but also align with your broader business strategy. With the right vending machines in place, you'll be well on your way to building a profitable and sustainable vending machine business.

Key Features to Look For

When it comes to choosing the right vending machines for your business, there are several key features that can make all the difference between running a smooth operation and dealing with constant headaches. By focusing on these elements, you'll not only ensure a more efficient business but also set yourself up for long-term success.

First and foremost, let's talk about the capacity of your vending machines. The capacity refers to the number of items the machine can hold at one time. This is crucial depending on the location and the type of products you plan to sell. High-traffic areas like malls or busy office buildings benefit from machines with larger capacities because they reduce the frequency of restocking. On the other hand, smaller venues might only necessitate machines with a lower capacity. Think of capacity as a balance between supply and demand that can save you both time and money.

Another feature to consider is the type of dispensing mechanism. Different vending machines use different methods to dispense products, and these mechanisms need to be reliable and durable. Spiral coils are common in snack machines, ensuring that each item is pushed forward when selected. Beverage machines often use conveyor belts or gravity-fed systems. Assessing the reliability and efficiency of these mechanisms can save you from frequent maintenance issues. Remember, a jammed vending machine isn't just an inconvenience—it's potential lost revenue.

User interface is another critical aspect. Modern machines come equipped with digital screens, touch panels, and user-friendly buttons. An intuitive interface can make a positive impression on your customers, making their purchasing experience smoother and more enjoyable. This could be the edge that makes customers choose your machine over another. Keeping the interface simple yet effective can also minimize user errors, thereby reducing complaints and downtime.

Payment options are evolving rapidly, and your vending machines need to keep up. While cash and coins have been traditional forms of payment, cashless options like credit cards, mobile payments, and even cryptocurrency are becoming the norm. Machines equipped with versatile payment systems not only attract more customers but also encourage higher spending per transaction. Given the increasing trend towards a cashless society, investing in machines that support multiple payment options is almost a necessity today.

Energy efficiency is an often-overlooked feature but can significantly impact your operating costs. Modern vending machines come with energy-saving modes, LED lighting, and efficient cooling systems. These features not only reduce energy consumption but also increase the machine's lifespan. Opting for energy-efficient models might involve a higher upfront cost, but the long-term savings and environmental benefits make it a wise investment.

Monitoring and inventory management systems are another technological advancement that can streamline your business operations. Machines equipped with remote monitoring capabilities allow you to track sales, inventory levels, and even technical issues in real-time. This means you can plan your restocking schedules more efficiently and address problems before they escalate. Investing in smart vending machines not only saves you manual labor but also provides valuable data that can help in making informed business decisions.

Security features are crucial to protect both your products and your revenue. Modern machines often come with reinforced exteriors, tamper-proof locks, and even surveillance cameras. Theft and vandalism can lead to significant losses, so ensuring your machines are secure can safeguard your investment. Additionally, insurance companies often offer lower premiums for businesses that take proactive measures against theft.

Customization options can also play a role in setting your business apart. Machines that offer customizable graphics and branding opportunities can be more visually appealing and can be aligned with your brand identity. This can be particularly useful if you have a specific theme or target audience in mind. Customization goes beyond mere aesthetics; it can also include specialized compartments for unique or delicate items, which can widen your product range and increase customer satisfaction.

Maintenance ease is another factor to consider. Machines that are simple to clean and maintain can save you a lot of time and hassle. Look for features like detachable trays, easy-access doors, and self-diagnostic systems. These practical elements can significantly reduce the time it takes for servicing, allowing you to keep your machines up and running more consistently. The less time you spend on maintenance, the more time you can devote to growing your business.

Climate control is particularly important if you are vending perishable items like food and beverages. Machines should have reliable refrigeration units if you plan to sell cold drinks or snacks. Conversely, if you are vending hot drinks, make sure the heating elements are efficient and consistent. Proper climate control ensures the quality and longevity of the products you are selling, contributing to customer satisfaction and repeat business.

Finally, consider the machine's footprint and adaptability to different spaces. Depending on where you plan to place them, the size and shape of the machine can be a significant factor. Some places may have space constraints, making compact or modular machines more suitable. Machines that can adapt to various environments without a hitch offer an edge in versatility, allowing you to quickly respond to new opportunities or changing market demands.

By focusing on these key features—capacity, dispensing mechanisms, user interface, payment options, energy efficiency, monitoring systems, security, customization, ease of maintenance, climate control, and adaptability—you'll be better equipped to choose the right vending machines for your unique needs. Each of these features contributes to the overall efficiency, profitability, and sustainability of your vending machine business, turning your investment into a consistent revenue stream.

Selecting the right vending machine involves more than just picking the first available option. It's about understanding your business goals and matching them with machines that offer the greatest potential for success. With careful consideration and an eye for detail, you'll be well on your way to building a thriving vending machine enterprise that not only meets but exceeds your expectations.

CHAPTER 4:
SELECTING PRIME LOCATIONS

Successfully choosing prime locations for your vending machines can make or break your business. Imagine placing your machines where the foot traffic is constant, varied, and composed of consumers hungry for the convenience you offer. High-traffic areas like malls, hospitals, colleges, and office buildings are goldmines for vending machine placement. It's crucial to think strategically about where your target customers spend their time and are most likely to purchase a quick snack or beverage. Don't just stop at where people are; consider the timing and flow of foot traffic. Once you've honed in on potential locations, the next step is negotiating agreements with property owners. A mutually beneficial deal not only secures your spot but also enhances your long-term profitability and business relationship. Tackling location selection with careful consideration and strategy sets a solid foundation for achieving sustained vending machine success.

High-Traffic Areas

When it comes to placing your vending machines, high-traffic areas are non-negotiables. Think of these spots as the prime real estate of the vending business world. It's where you get the most eyes on your machines and the highest chance of converting foot traffic into sales. These locations are the lifeblood of your vending operation and can significantly impact your revenue.

Let's start with an easy-to-overlook but incredibly profitable spot: colleges and universities. Campuses are bustling hubs of activity with students, staff, and visitors moving around every day. Placing machines in student union buildings, libraries, and near dorms can yield impressive returns. Remember, these are individuals who crave convenience and often have limited time between classes.

Airports and bus terminals also make for exceptional vending machine locations. Travelers are often in transit, waiting for their next connection, and are more likely to look for quick snacks or drinks. This urgency can translate into multiple purchases, especially when there's little competition outside your machine.

Gyms and fitness centers present unique opportunities as well. Patrons of these spaces are usually focused on health and wellness, so stocking your machines with protein shakes, hydration drinks, and healthy snacks can cater directly to their needs. This targeted approach can lead to repeat customers who value the convenience of grabbing a refreshing drink or nutritious snack post-workout.

Another goldmine? Hospitals. These are places with a constant influx of visitors, patients, and staff. By placing machines in waiting areas, cafeterias, and near main entrances, you can serve a diverse audience. Think about stocking a versatile selection ranging from healthy options for staff to comfort snacks for visitors—all while being mindful of any dietary restrictions prevalent in such environments.

Malls and shopping centers are another popular choice. These places have high foot traffic, composed of shoppers who may spend hours browsing stores. A strategically placed vending machine offering beverages, snacks, or even small convenience items can attract people looking to make a quick purchase without interrupting their shopping flow.

Automated Wealth

Corporate offices and business parks serve as excellent locations, too. Employees often reach for quick snacks and drinks during their breaks. Partnering with office complexes to place machines in break rooms, lounges, or lobbies can lead to steady sales, especially if you offer a good mix of healthy and indulgent snacks.

Sports venues are another promising option. People attending games and events are likely to buy snacks and drinks. Although these locations can be more competitive and sometimes involve higher fees or revenue-sharing agreements, the volume of sales can often make it worthwhile.

Hotels and motels shouldn't be overlooked either. Guests looking for a late-night snack or a quick breakfast option will appreciate the convenience of a vending machine in the lobby or by the elevator on each floor. Your machine can become their go-to option, especially when room service is limited or non-existent.

Arcades and family entertainment centers draw crowds of all ages. Kids, in particular, are more likely to ask their parents for snacks, and a well-stocked vending machine can cater to these impulses. Keep in mind the power of visual appeal here—brightly colored machines with attractive signage can capture the attention of young audiences more effectively.

Don't discount the potential of high schools and middle schools. Students here have limited time during breaks and lunch periods to grab something to eat or drink. Offering appealing and reasonably priced options can make your vending machine a popular choice. Just ensure your offerings meet school regulations regarding nutrition and healthy choices.

Public transport hubs like subway stations and train stations are bustling places where commuters appreciate the convenience of grabbing a quick snack or drink on the go. Ensuring your machines are well-maintained and consistently stocked can turn hurried travelers into regular customers.

Retail stores are another consideration. While it may sound redundant given that stores already sell products, consider places like home improvement stores or large furniture stores. Customers spend extended periods shopping for large items and may not want to pause their shopping trip for a snack or drink. A vending machine located strategically within the store can fill that need seamlessly.

Lastly, amusement parks and outdoor recreational areas are excellent high-traffic locations. Visitors to these places often spend long hours there, and providing accessible vending options can enhance their experience, making their day out more convenient and enjoyable.

To maximize the potential of these high-traffic areas, negotiate well with property owners and aim for locations with both high visibility and heavy foot traffic. Keep in mind the seasonal fluxes in traffic, such as peak times during holidays or certain days of the week, and stock your machines accordingly. Remember that cleanliness and machine functionality are paramount; a machine that's always in working order is more likely to attract repeat business.

It's also essential to remain adaptable. Traffic patterns can shift, and the profitability of a location can change over time. Keep track of your sales data, and don't be afraid to relocate machines if certain spots don't yield the expected returns. Flexibility and keen observation can turn a good vending machine location into a great one.

In conclusion, selecting high-traffic areas for your vending machines can be the game-changer for your business. By placing your machines where potential customers naturally congregate and move about, you're essentially setting them up to be effortlessly discovered and frequently used. The convenience you provide through strategic placement can transform casual passersby into loyal patrons, significantly boosting your revenue.

Understanding the dynamics of different high-traffic areas and how they align with your target demographics is crucial. Tailor your offerings to meet the needs and preferences of the users in each specific location, and nurture relationships with property owners to secure and maintain these prime spots. Let this strategy be the cornerstone upon which you build your thriving vending machine business.

Negotiating Agreements with Property Owners

In the realm of selecting prime locations for your vending machines, negotiating agreements with property owners can be a pivotal step. When done skillfully, these negotiations can secure spots that maximize visibility and traffic, ultimately boosting your profitability. This process may seem daunting, especially for newcomers to the business, but armed with the right strategies, you can turn it into a straightforward and even enjoyable experience.

First, understanding the value of the location from the owner's perspective is crucial. Property owners want assurances that your vending machine will be an asset rather than a nuisance. They're likely thinking about foot traffic, potential revenue splits, and possible disruptions. Thus, approaching these negotiations with a mindset of mutual benefit can set the right tone. Highlight how your vending machine can offer added convenience to their visitors or tenants and potentially increase the value of their property.

Preparation is another key element. Before you even approach a property owner, do your homework. How much traffic does the area get? What kinds of businesses or residences are nearby? What are the typical hours of operation for neighboring establishments? By gathering this information, you arm yourself with data that supports why your vending machine will be a successful addition to their property.

When it comes to the actual negotiation, clarity is critical. Outline what you are offering succinctly: a quality vending machine that's well-maintained and stocked with products tailored to the demographics of the area. Discuss the logistics—frequency of restocking, maintenance schedules, and how you'll handle any potential issues like machine malfunctions or litter around the vending area. Providing this level of detail can assuage any concerns the property owner might have and demonstrate your professionalism.

Don't overlook the power of incentives. Offering a share of the profits, often called a "commission," can be highly motivating for property owners. Typically, commissions can range from 10 to 20 percent of the machine's gross sales, but this can vary based on the location's traffic and potential profitability. Being flexible on this point can sometimes be the deciding factor in securing a prime spot for your machine.

Additionally, be transparent about the contractual terms. You'll want to clarify the duration of the agreement, the conditions under which it can be terminated, and any renewal clauses. Transparency fosters trust, making the property owner more likely to agree to your terms. It's also wise to discuss any exclusivity clauses; for instance, you might negotiate to be the sole vending machine operator on the premises, ensuring that your competition stays out.

While negotiating, listening is just as important as presenting your case. Understand the property owner's concerns and needs. Are they worried about vandalism? Offer to install a security camera. Concerned about electricity costs? Assure them that modern vending machines are energy-efficient and will not significantly impact their utility bills. By addressing their worries with practical solutions, you make it easier for them to say yes.

Remember, flexibility can be your friend in these negotiations. Be willing to adjust your proposal based on the property owner's feedback. Maybe they want the machine placed in a specific location for better visibility, or perhaps they're interested in a shorter initial contract to "test the waters." Showing that you are willing to work with them can go a long way in building a strong, long-term partnership.

Once an agreement is reached, make sure everything is put in writing in the form of a contract. This document should be clear and detailed, covering all aspects of your arrangement. Both parties should review the contract thoroughly before signing. It's advisable to have a legal professional look over the agreement to ensure that your interests are fully protected and that the contract adheres to local laws and regulations.

Patience is essential. Negotiations might take time as property owners weigh the pros and cons of your proposal. Follow up politely and be persistent but respectful. Keeping communication open and cordial can nudge the decision in your favor. It's not uncommon for property owners to take weeks or even months to make up their minds, especially if they're unfamiliar with vending machine agreements.

In some cases, you might encounter objections or outright rejections. Don't be disheartened. Use these experiences as learning opportunities. Ask for feedback on why your proposal was declined and use this information to refine your pitch for future negotiations. Persistence and adaptability are key traits for any successful entrepreneur, and they're particularly crucial in the vending machine business.

Building strong relationships is a long-term game. Once you've secured a location, maintain it well, and ensure the property owner is satisfied with the arrangement. This ongoing rapport can not only help retain the location but also potentially open doors to additional opportunities. A happy property owner is more likely to recommend you to others, helping you expand your vending machine empire.

In conclusion, negotiating agreements with property owners is a blend of preparation, persuasion, and patience. By approaching these negotiations with a well-thought-out strategy, clear communication, and a willingness to compromise, you can secure prime vending machine locations that will set the foundation for your business's success. Embrace it as a collaborative effort where both parties can find value, and you'll find that these agreements pave the way for a thriving and profitable vending machine enterprise.

Chapter 5:
Understanding Your Market

Understanding your market is crucial to the success of your vending machine business. It's not just about placing machines randomly and hoping for the best; you need to know who your customers are and what they want. Identify your target demographics—are they office workers, students, or gym-goers? Each group has different needs and preferences. Analyzing your competitors also offers valuable insights. What products are they offering? Where are they located? Learning from their strategies can help you refine your own approach. Ultimately, knowing your market inside and out allows you to tailor your offerings, optimize locations, and differentiate your brand, setting you up for a thriving, profitable business.

Identifying Target Demographics

When diving into the vending machine business, the importance of understanding who your customers are can't be overstated. Identifying target demographics is not just about knowing who might walk past your vending machine but also about grasping the nuances of their preferences and behaviors. Your ability to accurately profile your target market can mean the difference between a thriving vending machine operation and a sluggish one.

First, let's get a grip on what "target demographics" entails. In essence, it's the segmentation of the market into various categories based on factors like age, gender, income level, education, location, and lifestyle. By recognizing these segments, you can align your vending machine offerings to better meet their needs. For instance, a machine placed in a gym would likely profit more from selling protein bars and electrolyte drinks than sodas and chips. The idea is to sync your product offerings with the demands and desires of the foot traffic around your vending machine.

Now, why does this matter? Think of it this way: If you were selling ice cream, you'd place your cart in the park on a sunny day, not inside a movie theater on a cold, rainy evening. The same principle applies to vending machines. If your target demographic is college students, then it would benefit you to locate your machines in or around campuses and stock them with affordable snacks and energy drinks. Conversely, if you're targeting office workers in a corporate environment, you might want to stock higher-end snacks, healthy options, and perhaps even some quick meal solutions.

Another aspect to consider is the depth of consumer insight you need. This goes beyond the basic demographic cut and delves into psychographics—understanding the values, attitudes, and lifestyles of your potential customers. For example, millennials are generally more health-conscious and tech-savvy than previous generations. They value convenience but also want ethically sourced and healthier snack options. By adding healthier snack options and perhaps even integrating a cashless payment system, you cater directly to their preferences.

To gather these insights, it pays to do your homework. Secondary data from industry reports, market research studies, and even social media trends can offer a wealth of information. For instance, surveys and focus groups can help you gather firsthand information about what people in specific locations want. Don't shy away from visiting existing vending machine locations, observing the types of people using them, and possibly even engaging in a conversation about what they wish was available. The key is to observe, listen, and adapt.

Moreover, it's not just about what people want, but also when they want it. Understanding the behavior patterns of your target audience can guide restocking schedules. School locations, for instance, might see peak activity during early mornings, lunch breaks, and just after school ends. Conversely, a vending machine in a 24-hour gym might need checking early in the morning or late at night to cater to different exercise routines.

Location and demographics often go hand-in-hand. High-traffic areas like train stations, airports, and shopping malls serve a diverse crowd, making them excellent for machines that offer a variety of options. However, specialization could yield higher returns in niche markets. Residential buildings, especially in upscale communities, may benefit from premium offerings. On the other hand, industrial parks could see high demand for energy drinks and hearty snacks that workers prefer during their breaks.

Don't overlook cultural differences either. If you're planning to place machines in a culturally diverse area, understanding dietary restrictions and preferences is crucial. For instance, introducing halal or kosher snack options could endear you to specific demographic segments, enhancing customer satisfaction and loyalty.

In this journey, analytics will become your best friend. Modern vending machines equipped with smart technology can track sales data, providing insights into which products are flying off the shelves and which ones are gathering dust. This data-driven approach allows for real-time adjustments to stock, ensuring your vending machine remains attuned to consumer demands. For example, if data shows that a particular kind of granola bar is consistently selling out, that's your cue to stock more of it.

Demographic trends also fluctuate over time. The interests and preferences of Generation Z, for instance, are already proving to be different from millennials. Keeping a finger on the pulse of changing trends ensures your business remains relevant. Regularly updating product offerings based on seasonal changes, new health trends, and even new product launches can keep your vending machines a popular choice.

Leveraging social media can provide valuable insights too. Platforms like Instagram, Twitter, and Facebook are goldmines for understanding current trends. By observing which snack types are garnering likes and shares, you can make informed decisions about what to stock. What's more, actively engaging with users through social media polls or direct feedback can provide a more nuanced understanding of your target demographic's evolving tastes.

Finally, understanding target demographics is not a one-time task but an ongoing process. As neighborhoods evolve and consumer habits change, so too should your approach to stocking and placing vending machines. Regularly reviewing sales data, staying aware of market trends, and continually engaging with your customer base ensure that your vending machine business remains profitable and responsive to market demands.

To sum up, identifying target demographics requires a blend of demographic analysis, consumer behavior understanding, and market trend awareness. It's not just about pinpointing who your customers are but also about aligning your business strategy to meet and exceed their expectations. By investing time and resources into truly understanding your market, you'll set the foundation for a vending machine business that not only meets the needs of its customers but thrives by anticipating and adapting to ever-changing consumer demands. And with this keen insight, you'll be well on your way to creating a profitable, scalable, and deeply resonant vending machine business.

Analyzing Competitors

To thrive in the vending machine business, understanding and analyzing your competitors is crucial. Whether you're just starting or looking to scale your operation, gaining insights into who you're competing with and how they operate can make a significant difference. In this section, we'll delve into the importance of competitor analysis, how to gather relevant information, and how to use these findings to refine your strategy and outshine the competition.

First, let's consider why analyzing competitors is essential. Competitor analysis helps you identify market gaps, understand pricing strategies, and determine the strengths and weaknesses of other players in the market. It can also reveal trends and customer preferences that you might not have considered. By keeping an eye on your competitors, you'll be better positioned to make proactive changes and stay ahead of the curve.

Start by identifying who your competitors are. In the vending machine business, this includes both direct competitors—those who offer similar products and services—and indirect competitors—those who might not be in the vending business but still pose a threat. For instance, convenience stores, cafeterias, and even food delivery services could be considered indirect competitors.

Once you've identified your competitors, it's time to gather information. This process can be as straightforward or as detailed as you need it to be. Start with a basic overview: How many machines do they operate? Where are they located? What types of products do they sell? Are their machines updated with the latest technology? Keep your research organized by creating a spreadsheet or database to compile this information, which will make it easier to analyze later.

Dive deeper into the data by visiting the locations where your competitors' machines are placed. Observe the foot traffic and customer interactions. Note the condition of their machines—are they clean and well-maintained? Are they stocked with products that are in demand? Public reviews and social media mentions can also provide valuable insights into customer satisfaction and common complaints.

Analyze the pricing strategies of your competitors. It's crucial to understand where they position themselves in the market. Are they offering premium products at higher prices, or are they focusing on affordability? Pay attention to any promotions or loyalty programs they might be running. These strategies can provide clues about their target demographics and their overall business approach.

Customer service is another critical area to scrutinize. How quickly do your competitors respond to issues with their machines? Do they offer a customer service hotline? Are refunds handled smoothly? Excellent customer service can be a significant differentiator in the vending machine business, and understanding how your competitors manage this aspect can help you refine your own approach.

Technology is rapidly changing the vending machine landscape. Look at the technological features your competitors have adopted. Are they using smart vending machines with touchscreens, cashless payment options, or even remote inventory management? Technology not only enhances customer experience but also improves operational efficiency. Understanding the tech trends your competitors are embracing can guide your decisions on which innovations to integrate into your own business.

Next, consider the products stocked by your competitors. Take note of both the variety and quality. Are they offering niche items or sticking to traditional snacks and beverages? Do they rotate their product offerings to keep up with changing trends and seasons? The information you gather here can inform your own product mix and help you stand out by offering something unique.

Understanding the relationships your competitors have with suppliers can also offer valuable insights. If your competitors are getting better prices or exclusive products from certain suppliers, it might be worth exploring those relationships for your own benefit. Networking within industry circles can help you uncover these connections and potentially negotiate better deals.

While gathering all this information, make sure to analyze it through the lens of your business goals. Every competitor's strength can highlight an opportunity for you to differentiate. If a competitor's machines are always stocked but they lack the latest payment technology, consider investing in tech upgrades. If their customer service is slow, focus on offering quick and efficient service to your own customers.

Your analysis should also look at the operational aspects of your competitors' businesses. How often do they restock their machines, and what is their approach to maintenance? Efficiency in these areas can significantly impact profitability. Look for patterns and best practices that can be adapted to improve your own operations.

Regularly updating your competitor analysis is just as important as conducting it initially. The vending machine market is dynamic, with new entrants and exiting players altering the landscape regularly. Keep track of any significant changes in your competitors' strategies, such as new product introductions or shifts in pricing. These updates will help you stay responsive and agile in your strategic planning.

Identifying the market gaps left by competitors can offer golden opportunities for your vending machine business. Unmet needs, overlooked locations, and underserved demographics are potential goldmines waiting to be tapped. Use your analysis to focus on these areas; whether it's introducing healthier snack options in areas dominated by sugary treats or placing machines in locations that your competitors have neglected, filling these gaps can set you apart.

Finally, competitor analysis should be an ongoing process. Make it a part of your regular business routine to monitor shifts and trends within the market. Stay informed by attending industry events, subscribing to trade publications, and participating in online forums. Constant vigilance will keep you ahead of the curve, allowing you to adapt swiftly to changes and stay competitive.

In conclusion, analyzing competitors in the vending machine business is not a one-time task but a continuous effort. The information you gather can be a powerful tool in shaping your business strategy, improving your operations, and positioning yourself effectively in the market. By understanding who you're up against and leveraging this knowledge, you're well on your way to building a thriving and profitable vending machine business that stands out from the crowd.

Chapter 6: Building Your Brand

Building a solid brand is crucial for distinguishing your vending machine business in a crowded market. Think of your brand as the personality and promise of your business; it's what customers will remember and return to often. Start by brainstorming a memorable brand name that hints at your core values and vision—something catchy yet professional. Once you've nailed the name, designing a visually appealing logo and other branding materials like business cards and flyers will solidify your presence. Make your branding cohesive and consistent across all platforms, whether it's on your machines, website, or social media. The goal is to create an exceptional experience that resonates with your target audience and retains their loyalty. Developing a strong brand identity not only attracts new customers but also cements your reputation as a reliable and quality-focused business in the vending industry.

Creating a Memorable Brand Name

Creating a memorable brand name is a pivotal step in building your vending machine business. It's more than just a name—it's the first impression, the handshake, and often the deciding factor that sets you apart from countless competitors. A striking brand name can evoke curiosity, instill trust, and linger in the minds of potential customers and partners.

Imagine walking down a busy street. You're surrounded by an array of vending machines, but one catches your eye due to its compelling name—something that speaks to you, maybe even makes you smile. That's the magic we're aiming for. The name needs to be catchy and memorable, but it should also communicate what your business is about. It should encapsulate the values, quality, and uniqueness of what you offer.

First off, keep it simple. Overly complex names or ones that are difficult to pronounce will likely get lost in the noise. A good rule of thumb is that if a fifth-grader can easily spell it and say it, you're on the right track. Simplicity enhances recall, which is essential for any successful brand.

Secondly, your brand name should resonate with your target market. Are you catering to busy professionals in office buildings? Or maybe you've set up in schools, targeting students? Understanding who you're aiming to serve can help refine choices. For example, a name like "SnackHub" might appeal to tech-savvy office workers, whereas "FreshSchoolSnacks" could connect better with a younger, school-going audience and their guardians.

Moreover, consider the tone and feel of your name. Do you want it to sound fun and playful, or does professional and reliable suit your business better? Aligning the tone with your overall brand strategy is key. A playful name like "Chomp Time" might work stunningly for a snack vending machine, but could seem out of place for a healthy options machine aimed at fitness enthusiasts.

Another technique involves using alliteration or rhyme. These linguistic tools can make names more engaging and easier to remember. Consider iconic brands like "Coca-Cola" or "Dunkin' Donuts." The repetition of sounds makes these names stick in your memory like glue. Applying similar principles could give rise to gems like "Vibrant Vends" or "Crunchy Corner."

Then, there is the question of relevance and vision. Your name should provide a hint about the type of products you offer or the experience you deliver. You wouldn't want a name like "Soda Central" if your vending machines are focused on salads and health foods. For a business focused on eco-friendly options, something like "GreenChoice Vends" might instantly communicate your commitment to sustainability.

In the digital age, domain availability matters. Before you get too attached to a name, make sure the corresponding domain is available. Ideally, you'd want a .com extension, given its universal recognition and credibility. The same goes for social media handles—ensure that your brand name can be consistently represented across various platforms. Consistency helps in building a cohesive image, which is crucial for brand recognition.

Additionally, trademarking your brand name is something you shouldn't overlook. Conduct thorough research to ensure your chosen name isn't already in use within your industry. The last thing you want is a legal battle over naming rights once you've already put time and resources into marketing and branding. It's wise to consult a lawyer to ensure that your name is legally protectable.

While brainstorming names, consider gathering feedback. You might have a few options you love, but gauging reactions from a small, diverse group can provide valuable insights. Sometimes, what seems perfect to you may not click with others or may have unforeseen connotations.

An interesting aspect is the emotional connection your name can forge. Names that invoke positive emotions can create a subconscious pull towards your brand. Take "HappySnacks" for instance—this name suggests joy and satisfaction, appealing on an emotional level and creating a positive association with your products.

Let's not forget cultural sensitivity. Ensure your name doesn't carry negative connotations or inappropriate meanings in other languages or cultural contexts, especially if you have plans to expand your business internationally. What sounds neutral in one language might be offensive or ridiculous in another. Conduct a comprehensive check to avoid these pitfalls.

Brand storytelling is another angle to ponder. Your name can serve as the anchor for a broader narrative about your brand's journey, mission, and vision. If you can weave your name into a compelling story, it adds depth and makes it more memorable. For instance, a name like "FirstPick Vends" could come with an engaging story about your meticulous selection of the best quality products.

Finally, it's important to remember that your brand name is just the beginning. It sets the stage but doesn't define you entirely. Consistent delivery on the promises your name implies—be it quality, convenience, or customer service—will ultimately build the trust and loyalty you strive for. Think of your name as a foundation—a sturdy base upon which the edifice of your successful vending machine business can confidently rise.

Choosing a memorable brand name is a journey filled with creativity and strategic thinking. It's your opportunity to stand out in a crowded market and make a lasting impression. By keeping it simple, resonating with your target demographic, ensuring relevance, checking availability, and being culturally sensitive, you can create a brand name that will pave the way for your success in the vending machine business.

Designing Logos and Branding Materials

Creating a strong brand identity is one of the most essential steps in establishing your vending machine business. At the heart of this process is designing logos and creating branding materials that not only differentiate your business but also leave a lasting impression on your customers. Your logo and branding will be the visual representation of your company and can significantly impact how potential customers perceive your vending services. Let's dive into how you can create an unforgettable brand image.

Start by understanding the essence of your vending machine business. What values do you prioritize? Is your focus on convenience, healthy options, or luxury products? Your logo should encapsulate this essence. For instance, if you're emphasizing health, vibrant greens and clean lines might be suitable choices. Conversely, a luxury vending service might utilize sleek fonts and metallic colors. Remember, your logo is often the first impression customers will have of your brand, so it's crucial to make it count.

When designing your logo, simplicity is key. A logo doesn't need to be complex to be effective. In fact, some of the most iconic logos in the world are extremely simple (think Apple's apple or Nike's swoosh). Your logo should be easily identifiable and memorable. This means it should be versatile enough to look good across various platforms and mediums, whether it's emblazoned on a vending machine, featured on a website, or printed on business cards and flyers.

Collaboration with a skilled graphic designer can be invaluable in this process. While there are online tools and resources that allow for DIY logo creation, a professional designer brings expertise in color theory, typography, and design principles that can take your logo from good to great. They can also ensure that your logo is scalable and functional in both color and black-and-white formats, which is essential for different branding materials.

Once your logo is solidified, the next step is developing complementary branding materials. This includes business cards, flyers, brochures, and even your machine's decals. Consistency is crucial here; you want to establish a cohesive look and feel across all your materials.

This includes using the same color palette, fonts, and design elements. For example, if your logo features a specific shade of blue, that color should be prominent in your branding materials.

Don't overlook the power of typography. The fonts you choose will convey a lot about your brand. Modern, sans-serif fonts might suggest simplicity and efficiency, whereas serif fonts can denote tradition and reliability. Using a limited number of fonts will help in maintaining a clean, professional appearance across your materials.

Besides physical materials, digital branding elements are equally important. Your website, social media profiles, and even email templates should reflect your brand identity. Consistent branding in your digital presence will make your business appear professional and trustworthy. It's advisable to create a brand style guide that details all these elements, so anyone working on your marketing materials knows exactly what to use.

Brand storytelling can add another layer of depth to your logo and branding materials. Creating a narrative around your brand—whether it's about the origin story of your business, your commitment to quality, or anecdotes about customer satisfaction—can make your brand more relatable and memorable. People connect with stories, and weaving your story into your brand materials can set you apart from the competition.

In a competitive market like vending machines, where products can be quite similar, your brand's personality and aesthetic can be a deciding factor for customers. A vending machine with a well-branded, eye-catching design will stand out more than a generic, unbranded one. This visibility can attract more foot traffic and potentially lead to higher sales.

Creating branded swag can also be an effective strategy. Items like branded reusable water bottles, tote bags, and keychains can serve as constant reminders of your business. When customers use these items, they become walking advertisements for your brand, extending your reach without additional advertising costs.

Additionally, consider the environmental and ethical implications of your branding materials. Sustainable practices are not just trendy but also reflect well on your brand's integrity. Using recycled paper for your brochures or eco-friendly inks for your prints can appeal to environmentally conscious consumers. It shows that your brand is responsible and forward-thinking.

As you design your logos and branding materials, it's important to take a step back and critically evaluate their effectiveness. Do they communicate your core values? Are they visually appealing? Do they set you apart from competitors? Seek feedback from a diverse group of people, including potential customers, industry peers, and design professionals. Their insights can be invaluable for fine-tuning your brand's visuals.

Building your brand is an ongoing process. As your business evolves, your branding may need to adapt. This doesn't mean frequent overhauls, which can confuse customers, but subtle updates and refreshes can keep your brand current and relevant. Think of big brands like Pepsi or Starbucks; their logos have evolved over the years while retaining the essence that makes them recognizable.

Finally, understand the legal aspects of your branding. It's crucial to ensure that your logo and brand materials do not infringe on any existing trademarks. Once your designs are finalized, it's wise to trademark your logo and any distinctive branding elements to protect your intellectual property.

Designing logos and branding materials is more than just a creative endeavor; it's a strategic one. Done right, it serves as the foundation of your business's identity, helping you attract and retain customers in an increasingly competitive vending machine market. Invest the time and resources needed to get this aspect of your business right, and it will pay dividends in the long run, setting the stage for your vending enterprise's success.

Chapter 7: Sourcing Products

Once you've picked the perfect vending machines and secured high-traffic locations, the next critical step is sourcing products. This might seem straightforward, but it requires thoughtful consideration to ensure your machines are stocked with items that will sell. First, it's crucial to identify reliable suppliers who can deliver consistent quality and competitive pricing. Partnering with well-established vendors minimizes risks such as stock outages or subpar products. Equally important is your product mix. Think carefully about your target customers—are they kids looking for snacks, office workers needing a quick energy boost, or health-conscious gym-goers? A strategic approach to product selection can significantly impact your sales. Balancing popular, high-turnover items with niche products can cater to diverse tastes and maximize your profit margins. In essence, effective product sourcing is all about aligning your inventory with your audience's preferences while ensuring reliability and cost-effectiveness.

Finding Reliable Suppliers

Finding reliable suppliers is one of the most critical steps in building a successful vending machine business. It's the backbone that ensures your machines are stocked with high-quality, in-demand products for your customers. A reliable supplier will help you maintain a consistent supply chain, which is essential for maximizing sales and customer satisfaction.

Before diving into the specifics, it is vital to understand what makes a supplier reliable. A reliable supplier consistently delivers goods on time, provides high-quality products, and offers competitive pricing. They should also have a good track record of communication and be responsive to your needs and issues. Establishing a clear set of criteria for evaluating suppliers can save you time and prevent potential headaches down the line.

One of the first steps in finding trustworthy suppliers is doing thorough research. Start by leveraging online resources like supplier directories, trade associations, and industry forums. These platforms often provide reviews and ratings from other business owners, which can be invaluable in your decision-making process. Utilize search engines and social media platforms to look up potential suppliers and gather as much information as possible.

Networking is another fantastic way to find reliable suppliers. Attend industry trade shows, vending expos, and business networking events. These gatherings offer a unique opportunity to meet suppliers face-to-face, ask questions, and get a feel for their reliability. You may also find it beneficial to join industry associations where you can get recommendations from fellow vending machine business owners.

Recommendations and referrals can be very powerful. Talk to other business owners within the vending machine industry. Whether it's through formal networking events or casual conversations, other entrepreneurs can provide valuable insights based on their own experiences with suppliers. A personal recommendation often carries more weight than online reviews because it comes from someone who has already navigated the challenges you might face.

Once you've identified a list of potential suppliers, it's time to vet them thoroughly. Start by reaching out and initiating a conversation. Ask for samples of their products and inquire about their terms and conditions, minimum order quantities, and delivery schedules. Samples are particularly useful as they allow you to inspect the quality firsthand and ensure it meets your standards.

Another critical aspect of vetting suppliers is examining their financial stability. A supplier who is financially unstable could pose serious risks to your business. Research the company's history, check their credit rating, and feel free to ask them for references from other clients. This due diligence helps ensure that your supplier will not suddenly fail to deliver due to financial issues.

When negotiating terms, strive for flexibility. Opt for suppliers who are willing to offer flexible terms that align with your business needs. For instance, in the beginning stages of your business, you might want a supplier who can handle smaller order quantities. As your business grows, you'll need someone who can scale their services accordingly. Flexibility in payment terms is also essential. A supplier willing to negotiate on invoices can ease your cash flow management.

Don't underestimate the importance of a robust contract. A well-drafted contract can prevent misunderstandings and protect both parties in the event of disputes. Ensure that your contract covers delivery schedules, payment terms, quality assurance, penalties for non-compliance, and any other critical details pertinent to your business. Having legal counsel review the contract before signing can save you from potential pitfalls.

Building a strong relationship with your supplier is equally crucial. Foster open lines of communication and make an effort to understand their business constraints and opportunities. Cultivating this relationship can result in better terms, priority service, and even insider tips on upcoming deals or new products. Remember, a reliable supplier wants to see your business succeed because your success translates to their success.

While it's essential to find reliable suppliers, it's also wise not to put all your eggs in one basket. Relying on a single supplier can make your business vulnerable to disruptions. Diversify your supplier base to ensure you have multiple options should one supplier fail to meet your needs. This strategic redundancy can be a lifesaver in times of unforeseen challenges.

Leveraging technology can also streamline your supplier management process. Contemporary supply chain management software offers features that can help you track orders, monitor stock levels, and manage supplier communications efficiently. This technological edge can give you real-time insights into your inventory, helping you make informed decisions swiftly.

Considering sourcing locally versus internationally is another important aspect. Local suppliers often provide quicker lead times and easier communication due to cultural and time zone similarities. However, international suppliers can sometimes offer more competitive pricing or unique products not available domestically. Weighing the pros and cons of each option based on your specific needs and resources is key.

Assessing the environmental and social responsibility of your suppliers might also align with your business values. More consumers today are becoming conscious of ethical sourcing. Partnering with suppliers who adhere to sustainable and ethical practices can enhance your brand's reputation and appeal to a broader customer base. Be sure to inquire about the supplier's practices and certifications in this regard.

Lastly, always keep an eye on evolving trends and continuously re-evaluate your suppliers. The market is not static; new suppliers emerge, and existing ones evolve. Periodically review your supplier relationships to ensure you're still getting the best value. Conduct regular performance reviews based on key metrics like delivery timeliness, product quality, and communication efficiency. Staying proactive in this aspect will keep your business agile and ready to adapt to changes.

In conclusion, finding reliable suppliers is a multifaceted process that requires diligence, strategic planning, and continuous effort. By thoroughly vetting potential suppliers, maintaining strong relationships, leveraging technology, and keeping an eye on market trends, you can build a resilient supply chain that helps your vending machine business thrive. The success of your vending machines hinges significantly on the products they offer, making the reliability of your suppliers critically important.

Choosing the Right Product Mix

Choosing the right product mix is essential to running a profitable vending machine business. It's more than just stocking your machines with snacks and drinks. It's about understanding your market, analyzing competition, and offering products that resonate with your target demographic. While vending machines' primary allure is their convenience, success hinges on the satisfaction of a diverse customer base. Let's dive into how to create an enticing product offering that maximizes profit and keeps customers coming back.

First and foremost, knowing your audience is crucial. Different locations will have varied customer bases, which influences product selection. For example, a vending machine in a corporate office will have different demands than one in a high school. Corporate offices might prefer healthier snacks, premium beverages, and possibly even tech gadgets. In contrast, students might be on the lookout for affordable, quick snacks and energy drinks. Understanding who will be using your vending machines sets the foundation for choosing products that sell.

Conducting market research helps you pinpoint exactly what your customers want. Surveys, focus groups, and even observing competitor offerings can yield valuable insights. What are the best-selling items in similar locations? Are there products people keep asking for but aren't available? Answering these questions helps you stay competitive and ensures your vending machines meet actual demand.

While analyzing market needs, it's also important to consider trends. For instance, there has been a growing shift towards healthier eating habits. Stocking items like low-sugar snacks, organic options, or gluten-free products can set your vending machine apart from others. However, traditional favorites like chips and sodas still hold a strong place, providing a balanced mix that appeals to both health-conscious individuals and those looking for a quick treat.

Seasonality can also influence product choices. In warmer months, sales for cold beverages, ice cream, and other refreshing items tend to spike. Conversely, hot beverages and comfort snacks could see an uptick in colder weather. Rotating your inventory to match seasonal changes can keep your vending machine relevant year-round.

Then there's the question of variety versus focus. Should you offer a wide range of products or stick to a narrow selection? While variety can attract a broader group of customers, too many options might overwhelm and slow down decision-making. Keeping a focused selection can streamline restocking and simplify inventory management, potentially enhancing sales by reducing choice paralysis. Experimentation is key—monitoring sales data lets you refine your offering based on what works best for each location.

Product placement within the machine is another critical factor. Prime spots, such as eye-level shelves, should be reserved for high-margin items or best sellers. Lesser-known or new products can be placed in secondary positions but should still be easily accessible. Effective placement can significantly impact sales and customer satisfaction.

Don't underestimate the power of pricing in shaping your product mix. Competitive pricing strategies are crucial, especially if you're operating in areas with other vending machines nearby. It's a delicate balance—setting prices too high might drive customers away, while setting them too low can eat into your profit margins. Conducting a break-even analysis helps determine the ideal pricing that covers costs while still providing a good profit margin.

Supplier relationships also play a significant role in choosing the right product mix. Reliable suppliers can provide a consistent stock of high-demand items and may even offer insights into trending products. Building strong relationships with suppliers can lead to cost privileges, exclusive items, or promotional deals that can be an added advantage.

Moreover, flexibility and willingness to adapt can pave the path to success. Consumer preferences can shift quickly, and staying rigid can hinder your growth. Keep an eye on sales data, customer feedback, and market trends, and be willing to tweak your product mix as needed. Flexibility ensures that your vending machines remain a preferred choice amidst changing consumer trends.

Leveraging technology can aid significantly in choosing the right product mix. Modern vending machines often come equipped with smart technology that provides real-time data on sales and inventory levels. This data-driven approach allows you to see which products are performing well and which are not, enabling you to make informed decisions on inventory adjustments.

Another aspect to consider is product differentiation. In a crowded market, unique offerings can set your vending machines apart. Maybe exclusive local products, niche snacks, or limited-time offers can entice customers. Collaborating with local businesses to stock their products can also foster community relations and cater to regional tastes, giving you an edge over standard vending options.

Sustainability has become increasingly important to consumers. Stocking eco-friendly products or brands with a commitment to sustainability can attract a younger, more environmentally conscious demographic. Additionally, ensuring that the packaging for your snacks and drinks is recyclable or biodegradable can also win favor with customers and position your vending business as socially responsible.

Finally, staying attuned to industry developments can provide a competitive advantage. Keep up with trade magazines, attend industry events, and network with fellow vending entrepreneurs. This continuous learning approach keeps you informed about emerging products, new technologies, and best practices that can enhance your product mix and overall vending machine business.

In conclusion, choosing the right product mix is a dynamic process that requires ongoing attention and a keen understanding of your market. By thoughtfully selecting products that meet customer demands, staying responsive to trends, and leveraging technology, you can build a vending machine business that thrives and evolves with its customers' needs.

Chapter 8: Pricing Strategies

Pricing your products effectively is crucial for the success of your vending machine business. To set profitable prices, you'll first need to understand market rates and the cost of goods sold, ensuring your prices cover expenses while generating a healthy profit margin. Consider conducting a competitive analysis to see what other vending operators are charging for similar products, making sure to factor in location-specific factors. Testing different price points can help identify the sweet spot that maximizes revenue without alienating customers. Dynamic pricing, adjusting prices based on demand, location, and time, can also optimize profits. Ultimately, your pricing strategy should align with your overall business goals, whether that's rapid growth, market penetration, or maximized profitability. Remember, a well-thought-out pricing strategy is not just about numbers—it's about providing value to your customers while sustaining your business operations.

Setting Profitable Prices

Setting profitable prices for your vending machines is crucial for maximizing revenue, ensuring customer satisfaction, and staying competitive in the market. However, finding the sweet spot of pricing isn't always straightforward. It's a balancing act that requires understanding your costs, knowing your market, and being adaptable.

First and foremost, you'll need to calculate your costs. This includes the purchase price of the vending machines, maintenance costs, and, of course, the cost of the products themselves. Don't forget to account for additional expenses such as transportation, utility bills, and any leasing fees for the locations where your machines are placed. When you know your total costs, you can set a price that ensures you're making a profit while also offering value to your customers.

Knowing your market is the next vital step. Understand who your primary customers are, their spending habits, and what they perceive as a fair price. Demographics play a significant role here. For instance, a vending machine in a high school might have different pricing compared to one in a corporate office. Students might be more price-sensitive and volume-driven, whereas office workers might be willing to pay a premium for higher-quality snacks or drinks.

Another important factor is the pricing of your competitors. Take some time to scout out other vending machines in your target locations. What products are they offering, and at what price points? This information can provide you with a benchmark and help you decide if you should match, undercut, or even exceed their prices based on the unique value propositions you offer.

Now, let's talk about perceived value. It's not always about how much something costs to you; it's about how much your customers believe it's worth. Enhancing perceived value could involve offering brand-name products, healthier options, or items that are difficult to find elsewhere. If customers feel they're getting something exclusive or top-notch, they're likely to pay a bit more for it.

Experimentation is also key. Don't be afraid to adjust your prices based on how well products are selling. If an item is flying off the shelves, you might be able to get away with a slight price increase. Conversely, if something isn't moving, consider lowering its price or offering a deal, such as "Buy one, get one free," to incentivize purchases. The flexibility to adapt your pricing strategy is a significant advantage you have in the vending business.

Speaking of flexibility, seasonal pricing can be a strategic advantage as well. For example, cold beverages might sell better and can be priced slightly higher during summer months, while hot drinks may see increased demand—and potentially higher prices—during winter. Similarly, consider themed products during holidays or special events and adjust pricing accordingly.

Bundling products is another effective pricing strategy that can boost your profits. Instead of selling individual items exclusively, consider offering combo deals. For example, pairing a snack and a drink at a slightly discounted rate than if purchased separately can increase sales volume and customer satisfaction. Moreover, it can help you move lesser-demand items when bundled with popular ones.

It's also valuable to consider psychological pricing tactics. Techniques like setting prices at $1.99 instead of $2.00 can make a big difference. This minor change can often make a product seem more affordable while only slightly reducing your margins. Additionally, placing higher-priced items alongside standard-priced items can create a sense of value, pushing customers towards the moderately priced options that generate good profit margins.

While setting prices, it's essential to be transparent and maintain integrity. Customers appreciate honesty, and trust can go a long way in building a loyal customer base. Clearly display prices on your machine to eliminate any guesswork. You don't want to lose customers over a misunderstanding or deception.

Digital and cashless payments are becoming increasingly popular. If your vending machines support these payment methods, you can often justify higher prices. The convenience of not having to search for exact change adds an element of service that many are willing to pay a premium for. It's a small step, but it signifies that you are in tune with modern consumer expectations.

Lastly, regularly review your pricing. The market is dynamic, and what worked yesterday might not be as effective tomorrow. Monitor your sales data meticulously and be prepared to make adjustments. It's a learning process, and over time, you'll become better at anticipating what works best for your specific vending business model.

Setting profitable prices is a cornerstone of any successful vending machine operation. It involves a mix of understanding your costs, knowing your market, and being willing to experiment and adapt. By employing these strategies, you'll be well on your way to ensuring that your vending machine business remains profitable and competitive. Stick to these principles, and you'll likely find that sweet spot where your customers are happy and your business thrives.

Understanding Market Rates

When it comes to pricing strategies in the vending machine business, understanding market rates is pivotal. This knowledge isn't just about knowing what competitors are charging, but also involves a comprehensive understanding of the value perception of your products among your target customers. Market rates are essentially the average prices that customers expect to pay for certain products or services, and they can significantly influence how you set your own prices. For someone diving into the vending business, getting a grasp on these rates can make or break the profitability of your venture.

First, let's talk about gathering the right data. Conducting market research is a critical step. You need to get out there and observe what other vending machines in your target areas are charging. Visit high-traffic locations, check out the prices on a variety of items like snacks, drinks, and specialty products, and take note of which items seem to sell the most. Data collection can be done through simple observation or more structured approaches like surveys. Keep an eye on local trends and seasonal fluctuations too, as they can impact your pricing decisions.

The information you gather during your market research serves as a benchmark for your pricing strategy. However, analyzing this data to derive actionable insights requires more than just knowing the numbers. You need to understand the context—the demographics of the area, the types of competitors you're dealing with, and the specific needs and preferences of your potential customers. Are you targeting college students, office workers, or gym-goers? Each group has a different willingness to pay and expects different items from a vending machine.

Once you've got a handle on the market rates, the next step is to evaluate how your products fit within this landscape. Consider your product mix and the unique value you offer. Your pricing should reflect not only the cost of goods sold and your desired profit margins but also the perceived quality and convenience. For instance, if you're offering healthy, organic snacks in a fitness center, you can likely price them higher than you would in a regular office setting. Customers in a gym are willing to pay more for products that align with their health-conscious values.

It's crucial to remain flexible and adaptable. Market rates are not static; they fluctuate based on numerous factors, including economic conditions, consumer trends, and even technological advancements. Therefore, regularly updating yourself with the latest market information is essential. Use tools like market analysis reports, subscribe to industry publications, and network with other vending machine operators to stay informed.

Another key aspect to take into account is the negotiation with property owners and location managers. Often, the biggest expense in the vending machine business is not the products themselves but the commission and fees paid to property owners. These fees can drastically impact your pricing strategy and profitability. Before finalizing your product prices, make sure you understand the terms of your agreements and factor them into your overall pricing model. A higher commission fee might mean you'll need to price your products slightly higher to maintain your profit margins.

You also need to think about consumer psychology. Prices ending in .99 are a classic tactic, but there are more nuanced strategies to employ. For example, offering a small discount for buying multiple items can encourage higher sales volumes. "Buy two, get one free" or "bundle offers" are popular ways to increase the perceived value for customers, making them feel like they are getting a deal, even if they're spending a bit more overall. These subtle price tweaks can make a big difference in consumer behavior.

Investing in technology can also help you monitor and adjust your prices more effectively. Modern vending machines often come with built-in sales tracking and reporting functions. Leveraging these tools allows you to dynamically adjust prices based on real-time sales data. If a particular product isn't selling well, you can quickly lower the price to move inventory, or if demand is higher than expected, you can incrementally raise the price.

Don't overlook the importance of promotions and special offers. Limited-time discounts or seasonal sales can attract more customers and boost short-term sales. For instance, offering cold beverages at a slight discount during summer can push more volume. While these promotions might temporarily lower your margins, they can help you gain a loyal customer base that will continue to purchase from your machines even after the promotions end.

Consistency in quality and service is another aspect that indirectly impacts how you should understand and apply market rates. If customers know they can always get fresh, high-quality products from your vending machines, they are likely to pay a premium. On the other hand, if you often face stockouts or quality issues, you might need to lower your prices to retain customers, which is less than ideal for long-term profitability.

Lastly, always have an eye on the future. The vending machine industry is continually evolving, with new products and technologies emerging. Keeping abreast of these changes will help you anticipate shifts in market rates before they happen. Whether it's the introduction of cashless payment systems, new health and safety regulations, or emerging consumer trends like plant-based snacks, staying informed will position you better to adjust your pricing strategy proactively.

In conclusion, understanding market rates is a multifaceted endeavor that requires constant vigilance and a keen sense for the dynamics of your specific market. Combining empirical data with a thorough understanding of your customer base, competition, and broader economic trends will equip you to set prices that are both competitive and profitable. This approach will ultimately set the stage for sustaining and growing a successful vending machine business.

Chapter 9: Machine Maintenance and Troubleshooting

Taking care of your vending machines is crucial for ensuring they operate efficiently and remain profitable. Regular maintenance helps you avoid unexpected breakdowns, which can lead to lost sales and unhappy customers. Keep a schedule for routine check-ups, including cleaning interior components, checking for expired products, and verifying that all parts are functioning properly. When problems do arise, familiarize yourself with common issues like coin jams, card reader malfunctions, or refrigeration failures. Having a troubleshooting guide on hand can save valuable time and reduce downtime. Remember, a well-maintained machine not only performs better but also instills trust in your customers, knowing they can rely on your service. By being proactive and responsive in maintenance and troubleshooting, you're setting your business up for sustained success and growth.

Routine Maintenance Guidelines

One of the most critical aspects of maintaining a profitable vending machine business is ensuring your machines are in top working condition. Routine maintenance is not just about keeping things running; it's about preventing issues that could lead to downtime and lost revenue. Consistent care can save you time and money, plus keep your customers happy and coming back. This section will delve into practical, actionable maintenance strategies you can implement to ensure the longevity and efficiency of your vending machines.

First and foremost, cleanliness is paramount. Vending machines can get dirty quickly, attracting dust, grime, and sometimes even pests. Regular cleaning of both the interior and exterior is essential. Wipe down the machine's exterior with mild detergent and water. Avoid harsh chemicals as they can damage the material and affect the appearance. For the interior, make sure to clean the dispensing mechanisms and trays. Remove any residue or debris that might clog the machine. Consistent cleaning deters pests and presents a professional image to your customers.

Another core routine task is checking and refilling stock. Don't wait until your vending machine is empty to restock. Frequent monitoring of inventory levels helps ensure that popular items are always available, reducing missed sales opportunities. Use a systematic approach, such as FIFO (First In, First Out), to manage your stock. This method ensures older products are sold first, maintaining freshness and reducing waste. Record keeping can be simplified using vending management software, which can track inventory and alert you when stock is running low.

Inspecting the payment systems is equally crucial. Whether your machines accept coins, bills, or cards, these systems need to be in perfect condition. For coin mechanisms, check for jams or blockages and clear them immediately. Make sure the coin and bill acceptors are calibrated correctly to prevent rejection of valid currency. For card readers, ensure the connection is stable and the software is up-to-date. Malfunctioning payment systems can frustrate customers and lead to lost sales.

Lubrication of mechanical parts is often overlooked, yet it is vital for reducing wear and tear. Mechanical parts like gears, motors, and dispensing mechanisms benefit from regular lubrication. Check your machine's manual for the recommended type of lubricant and apply it as directed. Over-lubrication can attract dirt and dust, so it's crucial to get this right. Properly lubricated parts operate smoothly, extending the life of the machine and reducing the likelihood of breakdowns.

The refrigeration unit, if your vending machine has one, deserves special attention. Regularly clean the condenser coils to ensure efficient operation. Dust and dirt can accumulate on the coils, making the refrigeration unit work harder and consume more energy. Cleaning the coils can be done with a vacuum cleaner or a soft brush. Additionally, check the temperature settings to make sure they're optimal for the products you're selling. A faulty refrigeration unit can result in spoiled products and a bad customer experience.

Lighting also plays a role in the functionality and appeal of your vending machine. Check all bulbs and replace any that are burned out. Well-lit machines are more inviting and easier to use, especially in dimly lit locations. LED lights are a great option as they are long-lasting and energy-efficient.

Regularly checking and updating software is another essential aspect of maintenance. Many modern vending machines come with software that manages sales data, inventory levels, and payment processing. Keeping this software up-to-date ensures that you have the latest features and security updates. Regular updates can also fix bugs and improve the overall performance of your machine. Set a routine schedule to check for software updates from the manufacturer.

A proactive approach to maintenance includes regular functionality checks. Perform a comprehensive test of the machine's dispensing and payment functionalities at least once a month. Dispense all the different products to ensure there are no mechanical issues and that each selection works as it should. Simulate a transaction to confirm the payment system is working correctly. These tests help identify any potential issues before they become significant problems.

Keeping comprehensive records of your maintenance activities can be immensely beneficial. Document each task performed, the date it was completed, and any observations. These records help you track the health of your machines over time and can be invaluable when diagnosing recurring issues. Organized records also assist when handing over tasks to team members or when selling the business, providing a clear history of the machine's upkeep.

Customer feedback should not be underestimated as a tool for maintenance. Encourage your customers to report any issues they encounter with the vending machine. Provide easy ways for them to contact you, such as a phone number or email address displayed on the machine. Take their feedback seriously and address reported issues promptly. Customer reports can sometimes alert you to problems before you're even aware of them, helping you to rectify the situation quickly.

Developing a consistent schedule is fundamentally crucial for routine maintenance. Whether it's daily, weekly, or monthly tasks, sticking to a calendar ensures nothing is forgotten. Daily checks might include quick visual inspections and cleaning, while weekly tasks could involve stock checks and minor repairs. Monthly tasks may include more detailed inspections and functionality tests. A well-planned schedule allows you to stay on top of maintenance without becoming overwhelmed.

For those new to the vending business, partnering with a maintenance service can be a good investment. These professionals can provide regular servicing, ensuring that your machines are always in top condition. They can also train you on basic maintenance tasks, making you more self-sufficient over time. The cost of these services can be offset by the increased uptime and customer satisfaction, leading to higher profitability.

Lastly, it's essential to stay informed about the newest maintenance techniques and industry standards. Attending industry workshops, training sessions, and staying updated with trade publications can improve your skills and knowledge. As the saying goes, "An educated entrepreneur is a successful entrepreneur." Implementing the latest practices will give you a competitive edge and ensure your vending machines are always in excellent working condition.

Routine maintenance may seem time-consuming, but the benefits far outweigh the effort involved. Well-maintained machines operate more efficiently, last longer, and keep your customers happy, ultimately contributing to the success and profitability of your vending machine business. By implementing the guidelines discussed, you can avoid many common pitfalls and ensure that your venture is not just surviving but thriving.

Common Problems and Solutions

Running a vending machine business can be incredibly profitable, but it's not without its challenges. One of the most crucial aspects of keeping your business operational and profitable is understanding how to maintain and troubleshoot your vending machines effectively. This section will cover some common problems you might encounter and offer practical solutions to keep your machines running smoothly.

Power Issues

One of the most common issues vending machine operators face is power problems. You'll find that a machine can sometimes lose power or malfunction due to electrical issues. If your machine isn't powering on, the first step is to check the outlet. Ensure it's plugged in securely and that the outlet is functioning correctly by testing it with another device. Tripped circuit breakers are also frequently the culprit; reset them and see if the machine comes back to life.

If the issue isn't resolved by these basic checks, it might be a faulty power cord or internal wiring. Replacing a power cord is simple and cost-effective, but for internal wiring issues, you should consult a professional technician to avoid further damage or potential safety hazards.

Coin and Bill Jams

Another frequent problem is jams in the coin and bill acceptors. Coins and bills can get stuck, especially if they're worn out or damaged. To fix this, first, switch off your machine and then carefully remove the jammed coin or bill. Many vending machines have a release mechanism you can use to clear a jam without opening the machine fully. If not, you may need to open the coin/bill acceptor unit for a more thorough cleaning.

Keeping the acceptors clean and regularly servicing them can minimize the frequency of jams. Use a soft brush and canned air to clean these areas gently. Ensure the coins and bills you're accepting are in good condition as well. Old, damaged currency should be replaced regularly.

Dispensing Problems

Dispensing problems can make or break your customer experience. Sometimes, products don't dispense correctly, which could be due to several reasons, like misaligned spirals or blocked chutes. Start by examining whether the spiral mechanisms are working correctly. Turn off the machine, then manually rotate the spirals to see if they move freely. If they don't, adjust their position and ensure they're not obstructing one another.

Blocked chutes are another common culprit. Check if any products are stuck in the dispensing chute and remove them. Regular maintenance, including clearing debris and ensuring products are loaded correctly, will go a long way in preventing these issues.

Refrigeration Failures

For machines that vend cold beverages or perishable items, maintaining the refrigeration unit is critical. If the refrigeration unit fails, it could result in spoiled products, leading to losses. Start with the basics: check the thermostat settings, clean the condenser coils, and ensure the door seals are intact. Sometimes, a simple setting adjustment or cleaning can get your refrigeration unit back on track.

More complex issues, like refrigerant leaks or compressor problems, will likely require professional attention. Regularly scheduled servicing by a qualified technician can prevent such failures, ensuring that the cooling systems remain operational.

Network Connectivity Issues

Modern vending machines often rely on network connectivity for various functions, such as cashless payments and inventory tracking. Issues with connectivity can affect these capabilities, making it essential to address them promptly. First, check if the network modem is connected and powered on. Resetting your modem can sometimes resolve connectivity issues.

Make sure that any SIM cards or Wi-Fi modules are properly installed. If you're still facing issues, consult your network service provider for further assistance. Sometimes, updating the machine's firmware can fix connectivity problems, so ensure your vending machine's software is up-to-date.

Inventory Management Challenges

Keeping track of inventory is crucial for a vending machine business. Running out of stock can disappoint customers, while overstocking can tie up your capital. Inventory management software can help streamline this process. If you're experiencing discrepancies between your software and actual inventory, the issue could lie in data entry errors or system glitches.

Regularly audit your inventory manually to ensure the software is working correctly. Employ barcodes or RFID tags to automate the tracking process, reducing the chances of human error. Proper training for staff on how to use inventory management systems also helps to mitigate these issues.

Customer Service Complaints

Customer complaints are inevitable but can be a valuable source of feedback to improve your service. Common complaints often revolve around machine malfunctions, refunds, or product availability. Create a straightforward and effective process for dealing with complaints. Whether through a hotline, email, or a quick response QR code on the machine itself, make it easy for customers to reach out.

Address complaints promptly and take corrective measures to prevent recurrence. Happy customers can turn into loyal patrons, so view complaints as opportunities for improvement rather than nuisances.

Vandalism and Theft

Unfortunately, vandalism and theft are real risks in the vending machine business. Machines placed in high-traffic areas or poorly lit regions are particularly vulnerable. Invest in robust machines with strong locks and timers that limit access during off-hours. Surveillance cameras can also act as a deterrent and help identify culprits if an incident does occur.

Location choice is a critical factor in minimizing these risks. Partner with property owners to ensure your machines are in secure, well-monitored areas. Routine inspections and maintenance will also reveal if a machine has been tampered with, allowing you to address the issue before it becomes a significant problem.

Legal Compliance Issues

Ensuring that your vending machines comply with local laws and regulations is crucial to avoiding legal troubles. These can include health and safety regulations, ADA compliance, and business licensing requirements. It's essential to stay informed about the legal requirements specific to your area.

If you're unsure about any regulations, consult legal experts or industry consultants who specialize in vending machine businesses. Regularly review compliance standards and update your machines or business practices accordingly to avoid penalties and ensure smooth operations.

By understanding these common problems and their solutions, you're well on your way to running an efficient, profitable vending machine business. Regular maintenance and staying proactive about potential issues can save you from a lot of headaches down the line. Keep these tips in mind, and your vending enterprise will stand strong against these common hurdles.

Chapter 10:
Marketing Your Vending Business

When it comes to marketing your vending business, a strategic approach is key to gaining exposure and driving sales. Start by leveraging the power of social media platforms like Instagram, Facebook, and Twitter, which allows you to connect with your audience in real-time, showcase your products, and announce promotions, generating buzz around your vending machines. In addition to your online efforts, don't underestimate the effectiveness of traditional marketing methods. Flyers, posters, and local newspaper ads can be indispensable when targeting specific communities or high-traffic locations. Networking with local businesses and participating in community events can also create valuable word-of-mouth recommendations. Remember, the more visibility you have, the higher the likelihood of attracting a diverse customer base, ultimately increasing your profits and ensuring the long-term success of your vending operation.

Utilizing Social Media

Welcome to the digital age, where social media isn't just a platform for sharing cat videos anymore. It's a powerful tool that can propel your vending machine business from obscurity to stardom. Leveraging social media effectively is crucial for modern entrepreneurs aiming to maximize their reach and engagement. To kick things off, it's essential to establish your presence on key social media platforms such as Facebook, Instagram, Twitter, LinkedIn, and even TikTok.

Starting with Facebook, create a business page that showcases your brand's mission, values, and offerings. This isn't merely a static page but a dynamic hub where existing and potential customers can interact with you. Populate this page with photos of your vending machines, updates on new locations, and any promotions you might be running. Make sure your contact information is easy to find; you'd be surprised how many business pages lack this fundamental detail.

Instagram is another visual platform where aesthetics play a significant role. Your Instagram profile should tell a story visually. High-quality photos and short videos highlighting the products in your machines can engage your audience. Use features like Instagram Stories and Reels to offer behind-the-scenes glimpses of your operations. This kind of content is gold for engagement as it humanizes your brand and shows the hard work that goes into keeping those vending machines stocked and operational.

Don't overlook the power of Twitter for real-time communication and customer service. Twitter can serve as an informal customer support channel where customers ask questions and you provide instant solutions. Use it to share short, compelling updates, or even customer testimonials. Hashtags, when used strategically, can expand your reach beyond your immediate followers. For instance, tagging your posts with trending hashtags related to your industry can attract more eyeballs to your content.

LinkedIn might seem like an odd fit for a vending machine business, but don't underestimate its potential for B2B interactions. Here, you can connect with property managers, corporate offices, and other potential business clients who might be interested in having vending machines installed in their facilities. Regularly posting articles, updates, and business milestones can establish your brand as a thought leader in the vending industry.

Now, TikTok may seem unconventional, but it's a burgeoning platform that offers unique marketing opportunities, especially if your target demographic includes younger audiences. Short, creative videos demonstrating the convenience of your vending machines or showcasing popular products can go viral, giving your business a significant boost in visibility. TikTok's algorithm often promotes local content, which can be extremely beneficial if your vending machines are geographically concentrated.

Consistent branding across all these platforms is not just advisable but necessary. Use the same logo, color schemes, and brand voice to ensure unified messaging. Consistency helps in building brand recognition, making it easier for customers to trust and remember you. When creating content, keep your target demographic in mind. Tailor your posts to address their needs and interests, whether that's an office worker looking for a quick snack or a gym-goer needing a protein boost.

Engagement is key. It's not enough to just post; you need to interact. Reply to comments, like posts, and engage in conversations. This two-way interaction can build a strong community around your brand. User-generated content is another valuable asset. Encourage your customers to share their experiences by tagging your business or using a branded hashtag. This not only creates free content for you but also fosters a sense of community and loyalty among your customers.

Paid advertising on social media platforms can amplify your reach beyond organic growth. Facebook and Instagram offer robust advertising tools that allow you to target specific demographics, locations, and even interests. Running well-crafted ad campaigns can drive more traffic to your vending machines, boost sales, and increase brand awareness. Remember, a small ad budget well spent can yield significant returns.

Email marketing complements your social media efforts and provides a direct line of communication to your customers. Use social media to capture email addresses through exclusive offers, promotions, or simple opt-ins. An occasional, well-timed newsletter can keep your audience informed and engaged. It's a subtle nudge reminding them of your presence without being intrusive.

Contests and giveaways can skyrocket your engagement levels. People love free stuff, and a well-promoted contest can generate buzz. Use platforms like Instagram and Facebook to run these campaigns, encouraging users to share your posts or tag friends. The viral nature of such activities can dramatically increase your visibility and attract new followers.

Collaborations and partnerships with influencers or local businesses can also be incredibly beneficial. Influencers today have a significant pull over their audiences, and a collaboration with the right influencer can introduce your brand to thousands of potential customers. Choose influencers whose audience aligns with your target demographic. Similarly, partnering with local businesses for cross- promotions can widen your reach within the community.

Evaluate your performance regularly. Social media platforms offer analytics tools that provide valuable insights into your posts' performance, audience demographics, and engagement levels. Use these analytics to fine-tune your strategy. What type of content resonates the most? Which platform is driving the most engagement? Use this data to refine your approach for better results moving forward.

Future-proofing your strategy involves staying updated with social media trends and algorithms. The digital landscape changes rapidly, and what works today might not be effective tomorrow. Subscribe to industry blogs, take online courses, or even hire a social media consultant to keep your approach fresh and effective.

Building a social media marketing strategy is not a one-size-fits-all task. It requires ongoing effort, creativity, and adaptation. By utilizing the power of social media effectively, you can significantly enhance your vending machine business's visibility, engagement, and profitability. Don't underestimate this tool; wield it wisely and watch your business flourish.

Traditional Marketing Methods

When it comes to marketing your vending business, traditional methods still hold significant value and shouldn't be overlooked. While digital marketing offers a range of innovative tools and channels, traditional marketing strategies provide time-tested effectiveness that continues to resonate uniquely with different customer segments.

For a vending business, the first and perhaps most powerful form of traditional marketing is word of mouth. People naturally talk about their experiences—good or bad—with a product or service they've used. To benefit from this, ensure that your vending machines are always well-stocked, clean, and functional. A positive user experience can turn your customers into avid promoters of your vending machines, spreading the word to their friends, family, and colleagues.

Print advertising is another effective traditional marketing method. Although digital media has taken center stage, print ads in local newspapers, magazines, and community bulletins can still reach a wide audience, especially within a specific geographical area. Keep your print advertisements simple but eye-catching, and offer a small incentive, like a discount coupon, to drive immediate interest and response. Additionally, distributing flyers and brochures in high-traffic areas or directly mailing them to nearby offices, schools, and residential complexes can help create awareness about your vending locations.

Another classic marketing strategy is to leverage local events and sponsorships. Whether it's a charity run, a school fair, or a community festival, these events present excellent opportunities to promote your vending business. Sponsoring a local event not only puts your brand in front of a large number of potential customers but also helps in building a positive reputation within the community. Set up a booth or a stand and offer product samples from your vending machines to entice people to try out what you offer.

Don't underestimate the power of outdoor advertising. Billboards, posters, and signage in strategic locations can generate substantial visibility for your vending business. Think of bus stops, train stations, and busy street corners where foot traffic is high. Invest in creative designs that grab attention and clearly communicate what sets your vending machines apart, whether it's the quality of the products, innovative features like cashless payments, or unique items not available elsewhere.

In-store promotions can also be incredibly effective, especially if you have vending machines placed in retail environments like grocery stores, gyms, or office buildings. Collaborate with the store owners to create promotional materials that highlight your machines. You could run a limited-time offer or a discount on specific items, encouraging customers to make a purchase. Near machine signage is crucial in these scenarios. Clear, attractive signs can make all the difference in informing potential users about your vending services.

Partnerships with local businesses can also amplify your traditional marketing efforts. For instance, you can team up with local cafés, restaurants, or bookstores to offer combo deals or exclusive offers that can attract their existing customer base to your vending machines. Cross-promotion can be a win-win situation, boosting business for both parties involved and fostering a sense of community collaboration.

Networking is another valuable aspect of traditional marketing. Attend trade shows, business networking events, and industry conferences to meet other entrepreneurs, potential clients, and suppliers. Building relationships in person can open doors to new opportunities and resources that can benefit your vending business in the long run. Always carry business cards and be ready to discuss how your vending solutions can add value to various locations and demographics.

Finally, traditional media coverage can significantly boost your exposure. Reach out to local newspapers, radio stations, and TV channels with press releases about your vending business. Whether it's launching a new machine, introducing an innovative product, or participating in a community event, getting media coverage can provide a credibility boost and reach audiences who may not be as active online. Personal stories or unique selling points can make for compelling media content, increasing the likelihood that your story will get coverage.

In conclusion, while the allure of digital marketing is strong, traditional marketing methods bring a balance of trust and community engagement that can be highly effective for a vending business. By combining these strategies with modern digital tactics, you can create a robust marketing plan that reaches a wider audience and drives sustainable growth for your vending business. The key is to be consistent, creative, and community-focused, always looking for ways to engage with your customer base through multiple channels and touchpoints.

Chapter 11: Legal Considerations

When diving into the vending machine business, navigating the labyrinth of legal considerations is crucial for long-term success. First, you'll need to secure the appropriate licenses and permits, which can vary based on your location and the types of products you plan to vend. Zoning laws are another essential aspect; they determine where you can place your machines and may have restrictions based on property usage or proximity to other businesses. Additionally, understanding contractual obligations—whether it's leases for machine placements or supplier agreements—can prevent future disputes and financial pitfalls. Ensuring compliance with health and safety regulations, especially if your machines offer food or beverages, is non-negotiable. A proactive approach to these legal details not only protects your business but also fosters trust and professionalism with your partners and customers.

Licensing and Permits

Jumping headfirst into the vending machine business can be incredibly exciting, but before you start placing machines around town, it's crucial to get familiar with local licensing and permits. These legal requirements are often the gatekeepers of your entrepreneurial journey, and ignoring them can result in hefty fines or even the shutdown of your operations. Let's explore what you need to know to navigate this maze with ease.

The first step in obtaining the necessary licenses and permits is to understand that the requirements can vary widely depending on your location. Municipalities, counties, and states each have their own set of rules and regulations. It's essential to contact your local government offices or visit their websites to get the most up-to-date information. Starting at the local level, you usually need a business license or a vendor license. This allows you to legally operate within a specific area and ensures that you're adhering to local business laws.

Now, let's talk specifics. If you're planning to place your vending machines inside another business's location, such as a gym or office building, ensure that your agreement with the location owner covers permissions and any necessary arrangements for local permits. Some states also require a sales tax permit. This helps the government track and collect sales tax on the goods sold through your vending machines. Typically, you'll have to file for this at your state's Department of Revenue or similar entity.

Moreover, if your vending machines dispense food items, there are additional layers of regulatory compliance to consider. Health department permits are usually a must if you're selling perishable goods like sandwiches, salads, or dairy products. These permits are designed to ensure that your vending machines meet local health standards, keeping both you and your customers safe. Regular inspections may follow once you have these permits, so maintaining high standards of cleanliness and food safety is non-negotiable.

For those planning to offer high-value items or specialty products, be aware that certain goods may come with their own set of licensing needs. For example, if you intend to sell alcohol, tobacco, or pharmaceuticals, there are specialized permits and licenses required. These often involve more stringent background checks and higher fees, but they are essential for legal compliance.

Financial outlays for licenses and permits can add up quickly, so it's wise to budget accordingly. When putting together your business plan, allocate a section of your budget specifically for these costs. They're an investment in your business's legitimacy and long-term success. Remember, skimping on legal fees now can lead to expensive penalties down the road.

Another critical aspect of licensing and permits is insurance. While not always legally mandated, carrying adequate insurance is prudent. General liability insurance will cover various potential issues, from customer injury at the vending machine to property damage. If you're dealing with perishables, consider product liability insurance as well to cover any claims related to food safety.

Besides individual licenses, some states may offer bundled permits. These "one-stop-shop" permits can simplify the process by covering multiple aspects of your operation under one license. Call your local licensing offices to find out if this option is available in your region. It can save you time, paperwork, and potentially even money.

Don't forget about renewing these licenses and permits. Most permits are not one-and-done affairs; they require annual or even more frequent renewals. Schedule reminders and consider setting up auto-payments if possible to avoid lapses, which can be disruptive to your business. Late fees and other penalties for expired permits can add unnecessary stress and financial strain.

Finally, consider professional help. While the DIY approach is admirable, the minutiae of local licensing and permits can be overwhelming and time-consuming. Hiring a lawyer or a consultant who specializes in local business licensing can streamline the process. They'll ensure you've covered all bases and can even assist with paperwork, allowing you to focus on other aspects of your business.

In conclusion, securing the proper licensing and permits is an essential foundation for launching a successful vending machine business. It might seem daunting initially, but with diligence and the right resources, navigating these legal waters becomes much more manageable. Armed with the proper permits, you can confidently place your machines, knowing your business is on solid legal ground.

Understanding Zoning Laws

As you venture into the world of vending machine businesses, one of the most critical aspects you'll encounter is zoning laws. Understanding zoning laws is essential to ensure you operate within legal boundaries and maximize your potential profit. Zoning laws dictate where you can place your vending machines and what types of products you can offer in certain areas. Ignoring these regulations can result in hefty fines, forced removal of your machines, and other legal headaches that can cripple your business before it even takes off.

First and foremost, zoning laws vary significantly from one jurisdiction to another. What might be permissible in one city could be strictly prohibited in another. Therefore, the first step in understanding zoning laws is to familiarize yourself with local regulations. Contact your local municipal or county zoning office to get detailed information on the rules applicable in your area. It may be helpful to speak directly with a zoning officer who can provide insights specific to vending machines.

Zoning laws are typically put in place to achieve a balance between various land uses—commercial, residential, industrial, and public spaces. When you think about where to place your vending machines, it's paramount to consider these zoning categories. For instance, commercial zones are generally more lenient and accommodating when it comes to vending machines, compared to residential areas where restrictions tend to be far stricter. Schools and recreational areas often have specific guidelines, so always verify beforehand.

Another crucial element to consider is how zoning laws intersect with the products you intend to sell. Certain areas may have restrictions on selling specific types of products, such as alcohol, tobacco, or even sugary snacks. For example, many jurisdictions have strict regulations regarding the placement of vending machines selling sugary snacks or soda near schools or children's playgrounds. Compliance with these product-specific zoning regulations not only helps you avoid legal trouble but also demonstrates a responsible business ethos.

One tactic to navigate zoning laws effectively is to leverage professional advice. Engaging a local attorney who specializes in commercial law can provide you with in-depth knowledge and actionable strategies to comply with the pertinent regulations. Legal advice early in your business planning process can save you time and money in the long run.

In some cases, zoning laws may not explicitly mention vending machines. This can pose both challenges and opportunities. Ambiguous laws can sometimes be navigated successfully by applying for special permits or variances. A variance is an authorized exception to the zoning regulations, often granted when compliance with the law results in undue hardship. To secure a variance, you usually need to present a compelling case to the local zoning board, demonstrating that your vending machine will not negatively impact the community.

Understanding the public sentiment toward vending machines in your target areas can be beneficial when dealing with zoning boards. Community support can go a long way in swaying decisions in your favor. Therefore, consider attending community meetings or engaging in local forums to build a positive reputation for your business.

In addition to local zoning laws, don't overlook other legal considerations that might affect your vending machine placements, such as building codes, health department regulations, and fire safety codes. Building codes may dictate where a vending machine can be installed within a facility, setting requirements on the proximity to exits or stairways to ensure they don't obstruct foot traffic. Similarly, health department regulations may come into play if you plan to sell perishable food items. These could involve regular inspections, hygiene standards, and storage requirements.

Fire safety codes might not be the first thing that comes to mind when placing vending machines, but they are equally crucial. For example, placing machines in narrow hallways or near fire exits could violate fire safety regulations. Such oversights can result in penalties or forced removals, bringing unexpected disruptions to your cash flow.

While navigating zoning laws might seem daunting, it's worth noting that these regulations exist for valid reasons, aiming to create harmonious communities and safeguard public interests. When leveraged appropriately, understanding and adhering to zoning laws can actually play to your advantage. For example, many municipalities might allow vending machines in commercial zones where there's high foot traffic but restrict them in residential areas. Placing your machines in high-traffic commercial zones will naturally give you access to more customers.

The process of securing permissions and licenses can be streamlined by building strong relationships with property owners and local businesses. Often, they have more experience dealing with local zoning issues and can offer invaluable advice or assistance. Transparency about your business intentions and a demonstrated commitment to complying with local laws can foster goodwill, making negotiations smoother and more effective.

In certain situations, zoning laws may align with larger urban planning goals, such as promoting healthier living environments. For example, several cities are increasingly pushing for the installation of vending machines that dispense healthy food options, especially in community centers, public parks, and healthcare facilities. By aligning your vending machine business with these objectives, you might not only comply with zoning laws but also tap into niche markets that are increasingly growing in demand.

An important aspect often overlooked is the role of technology in adhering to zoning laws. Modern vending machines equipped with smart technology can collect data and provide insights into the optimal placement of your units. They can track sales patterns, giving you a clearer picture of customer preferences and needs, which can be cross-referenced with zoning maps to identify the most legally and commercially viable locations for your machines. Utilizing such technology can give you a competitive edge and ensure you stay compliant with zoning regulations.

Keep in mind that zoning laws are not static; they evolve. Urban development plans, changes in local government policies, or shifts in community interests can result in updates to zoning laws. Therefore, it's essential to stay informed about any changes that might affect your vending machine locations. Subscribing to local business newsletters, joining relevant industry associations, or even setting up alerts for zoning law updates in your area can help you stay ahead of the curve.

Engaging in continuous education and training can be hugely beneficial. Many local business councils and chambers of commerce offer workshops on navigating local regulations, which often include zoning laws. These sessions can provide you with the latest insights and practical tips for compliant business operations.

Lastly, remember that while zoning laws can feel restrictive, they also offer a framework within which you can operate safely and legally.

They help ensure that your vending machines serve the community in a manner that is both beneficial and sustainable. Rather than viewing these laws as obstacles, consider them as guidelines that help you establish a reputable and trustworthy business.

By thoroughly understanding zoning laws, seeking professional advice when needed, and staying adaptable to regulatory changes, you'll be well-equipped to place your vending machines in the most favorable and compliant locations. This attention to legal detail not only secures your business operations but also builds a strong foundation for long-term success.

Chapter 12:
Financial Management

Successful financial management is the cornerstone of any profitable vending machine business. It all starts with setting up an efficient accounting system that lets you track expenses, revenues, and profits with ease. Managing cash flow is equally crucial; your goal should be to ensure that your income consistently exceeds your outgoings, allowing for reinvestment and growth. You'll want to develop a clear budget to cover operational costs, emergency repairs, and unexpected expenses. Regular financial reviews help you stay on top of your business's health and make informed decisions. Automation tools can simplify processes, but personal oversight is irreplaceable. Stay disciplined and proactive, and you'll lay the groundwork for lasting financial success in your vending venture.

Setting Up Your Accounting System

Starting a vending machine business is exciting, but without strong financial management, even the most promising ventures can flounder. Setting up your accounting system is a foundational step that you'll thank yourself for down the line. It's not just about crunching numbers; it's about providing a clear picture of your business's health, tracking expenses, and ensuring you're compliant with tax regulations. Let's break down the essential components you'll need to set up an effective accounting system for your vending machine business.

First things first: selecting the right accounting software is crucial. Many options are available, from straightforward, user-friendly systems like QuickBooks and FreshBooks for smaller operations, to more robust platforms like Xero for larger, multifaceted businesses. Your choice should be guided by your business size, the complexity of your operations, and your comfort level with technology. Whichever software you choose, make sure it offers features like expense tracking, invoicing, payroll processing, and compatibility with your bank for easy reconciliation.

Once you've chosen your software, it's time to set up your chart of accounts. This is essentially a list of all the financial accounts in your business, organized by categories like assets, liabilities, income, and expenses. In the context of a vending machine business, your accounts might include cash on hand, inventory, sales revenue, and repair expenses. Having a detailed chart of accounts helps keep your financial data organized and makes it easier to run reports and analyze the financial health of your business.

Let's talk about inventory management. One of the biggest expenses in a vending machine business is the cost of goods sold (COGS). Your accounting system should track inventory levels in real-time and record these costs accurately. This will give you insights into your business's profitability. For instance, if you notice that certain products sell faster than others, you can adjust your inventory purchases accordingly.

It's essential to separate your personal and business finances. Open a dedicated business bank account where all transactions related to your vending machine business will be conducted. This simplifies accounting and ensures that when tax season rolls around, you won't find yourself scrambling to separate personal expenses from business ones. Doing this will also provide a more professional appearance to anyone you do business with, whether they be suppliers or clients.

Why is record-keeping so crucial? Well, in a vending machine business, cash flow can be very dynamic, with daily sales that must be meticulously recorded. You'll want to keep daily records of each machine's earnings, costs for restocking, and any maintenance expenses. Use your accounting software to input these records regularly, allowing you to generate useful reports such as profit and loss statements, balance sheets, and cash flow statements.

When it comes to tax time, a precisely configured accounting system will be your best friend. Consult with a tax professional to understand which tax obligations your vending machine business will have and how to prepare for them. They can guide you on essential deductions and tax credits you might be eligible for, whether for equipment purchases or vehicle expenses used for service routes.

You should also establish a routine for regular financial check-ups. Set aside time weekly, monthly, and quarterly to review your financial reports. Weekly reviews can inform you about cash-on-hand and upcoming expenses, while monthly or quarterly reviews can help you make more strategic decisions, such as expanding to new locations or adjusting your product mix.

Don't underestimate the power of budgeting. If you plan to expand your vending machine operations, invest in new machines, or hire additional staff, creating a detailed budget will help you allocate resources wisely. Forecast your revenue and expenses over the next three to twelve months. By comparing actual results with your budgeted projections, you can quickly identify discrepancies and make informed adjustments.

Another key aspect is setting up a system for timely invoicing and collections. If you have partnerships or agreements with property owners, you must ensure you're billing them correctly and at the agreed-upon intervals. Timely invoicing paired with rigorous follow-up ensures that your cash inflows remain steady.

Additionally, consider the role of payroll management if you're employing staff to service the machines. Your accounting software should support payroll functions, including automatic calculations of employee wages, tax withholdings, and benefits. This not only minimizes errors but also ensures compliance with labor laws.

Finally, protecting your financial data is critical. Make sure that the accounting software you choose offers robust security features like data encryption and regular backups. If possible, utilize multi-factor authentication to add an additional layer of security. Partner with a certified IT professional to set up a secure infrastructure, especially if you plan to manage sensitive financial data on multiple devices.

In summary, setting up your accounting system is more than just a procedural step; it's an ongoing process that requires diligence, regular updates, and strategic planning. An effective accounting system will not only help you track your earnings and expenses but also provide invaluable insights into your business operations, paving the way for informed decision-making and long-term success. By taking the time to establish a resilient accounting system now, you're investing in the foundation upon which your vending machine empire will be built.

Managing Cash Flow

Managing cash flow in a vending machine business can determine whether your enterprise thrives or collapses. Indeed, cash flow management is essential to maintaining liquidity, paying suppliers, and covering operational expenses. For aspiring entrepreneurs and seasoned business owners, mastering cash flow management can provide a sturdy foundation for sustainable growth. Let's dive into the practical aspects of managing cash flow effectively.

Firstly, it's crucial to understand what cash flow is. Simply put, cash flow is the movement of money in and out of your business. While revenue refers to the money coming in from sales, cash flow is broader and includes all expenses like rent, supplies, and unexpected repairs. A positive cash flow means you have more money coming in than going out, allowing for savings, investments, or expansions. Conversely, negative cash flow signals trouble, where expenses exceed revenue, risking debt accumulation or worse.

Start by setting up a robust accounting system, ensuring you can accurately track income and expenses. Digital accounting tools like QuickBooks or Xero help you keep all financial records in one place, providing transparent insights into your cash flow status. Good accounting practices will help you generate clear cash flow statements, make informed financial decisions, and comply with tax obligations without the last-minute stress.

Another strategy is to categorize your expenses into fixed and variable costs. Fixed costs are consistent—like rental fees for locations or software subscriptions, while variable costs fluctuate with sales volume—like inventory restocking or utility bills. Understanding this distinction allows you to budget more accurately and prepare for lean periods, helping to maintain a positive cash flow year-round.

Timing also plays a pivotal role in managing cash flow. Perhaps your vending machines are in high traffic areas, predicting seasonal spikes and dips in sales can be game-changers. Offer promotions or limited-time discounts during slow seasons to boost sales, while ensuring you're fully stocked during peak times to maximize revenue. Predictability, as much as possible, in the vending world, helps maintain a balanced cash flow.

One of the underestimated tools in cash flow management is invoicing. Even though most transactions in vending machines are immediate, there might be scenarios where you invoice for bulk orders or service provisions. Streamlining your invoicing process ensures prompt payment and avoids gaps in cash flow. Automate invoicing where possible, using payment reminders and digital payment gateways to make it convenient for your clients to settle dues on time.

Cash collections from vending machines should be scheduled frequently. Depending on sales volume, determine a routine—daily, weekly, or bi-weekly—to gather money from machines. Regular collections not only prevent theft but also ensure that you have constant liquidity. While it might feel labor-intensive, consistency in this process translates to better cash flow visibility and immediate funds for operational needs.

Moreover, maintain a reserve fund, often called a cash cushion. Unforeseen circumstances like machine breakdowns or unexpected supplier price hikes can hurt your finances. Having an emergency fund ensures you won't disrupt your regular business operations and can continue to provide a high level of service. The cash cushion should ideally cover several months of expenses, providing a buffer during financial hiccups.

Don't overlook the power of negotiating with suppliers. Building a good relationship with your suppliers can result in better payment terms, discounts, and bulk-purchasing benefits, directly influencing your cash flow. For instance, negotiating extended payment terms can allow you to maintain liquidity while you turn inventory into sales. Similarly, taking advantage of early payment discounts can save substantial amounts over time.

An often-overlooked aspect of cash flow management is leveraging technology. Modern vending machines come equipped with telemetry systems that provide real-time data on sales, inventory levels, and machine health. These insights can be powerful tools for predicting cash flow fluctuations and restocking needs, ensuring you're never out of popular items and can optimize your cash inflow.

Consider diversifying payment methods. Cash is no longer king. Incorporating card payments, mobile wallets, or even cryptocurrency can attract a broader customer base, increase sales, and subsequently improve cash flow. Modern consumers prefer the convenience of cashless transactions, and vending machines that cater to this preference are likely to see a bump in revenue.

Generating passive income isn't solely about placing machines and waiting for revenue. It's also about strategically managing the money flow to ensure sustainability. For instance, reinvesting a portion of your profits back into the business—be it through acquiring more machines, upgrading technology, or exploring new locations—provides avenues for continuous revenue growth. Reinvestment ensures your business remains competitive and mitigates the stagnation risk.

Periodic financial audits are essential. They help detect discrepancies early, enabling corrective actions before minor issues snowball into significant problems. Hiring an accountant or financial advisor can provide the expertise needed for these audits, ensuring that every penny is accounted for, and your financial health remains robust.

Lastly, financial education is an ongoing process. The landscape of business and finance constantly evolves, and keeping abreast of the latest financial strategies, tools, and regulations can provide an edge over competitors. Books, webinars, and courses on financial management can significantly augment your understanding and capability in managing cash flow.

In conclusion, mastering cash flow management in your vending machine business can significantly enhance its profitability and sustainability. By leveraging technology, maintaining reserves, negotiating smartly, and staying continually educated on best practices, you can build a robust financial framework. This not only secures your business's immediate operations but also sets the stage for long-term growth and success. Always remember, a profitable vending machine business is as much about effective financial management as it is about strategic placements and quality products.

Chapter 13: Operations and Inventory Management

To run a successful vending machine business, mastering operations and inventory management is paramount. This involves not just tracking what goes into each machine but also understanding product turnover rates, which are critical to maximizing profits. Efficient restocking is key; you'll need a streamlined system to ensure popular items are replenished before they sell out, while less popular products are evaluated and potentially rotated out. Implementing inventory software can significantly reduce manual errors and save time. A well-maintained schedule for both checking your machines and updating inventory ensures you're always ahead of potential shortages and can pivot quickly in response to changing customer preferences. Ultimately, the goal is to maintain a seamless operation where your machines never miss a sales opportunity due to stock issues, setting you up for consistent, passive income.

Tracking Inventory

Tracking inventory is the backbone of any successful vending machine business. Without a robust system in place, you could find yourself facing stockouts, overstocking, or even financial losses. Keeping tabs on what's in your machines ensures that every slot is filled with products your customers want, reducing downtime and increasing your bottom line.

Firstly, it's crucial to set up a reliable system for monitoring your inventory levels. Traditional methods involve manually counting items during each service visit. While this has worked for many operators, the advent of technology offers more efficient solutions. Inventory management software specifically designed for vending machines can sync with your operations, providing real-time data on stock levels, sales patterns, and shelf life. This enables you to make informed decisions swiftly.

Investing in modern vending machines equipped with telemetry systems can significantly simplify your inventory tracking process. These machines communicate directly with your software, updating stock levels every time a product is sold. Imagine never having to guess if you need to restock a particular item—it's all right there at your fingertips. This data can also help identify best-sellers and slow movers, allowing you to adapt your product mix based on actual demand.

Another critical aspect of tracking inventory is understanding your sales cycles. Does your machine sell more snacks during the workweek and more drinks over the weekend? Identifying these patterns can help you plan your restocking schedule more effectively. For instance, if you notice a spike in beverage sales around the middle of the week, you can make sure to stock up on those items on Tuesday. Recognizing these trends could mean the difference between a sold-out machine and one that is continually stocked to meet demand.

Don't overlook the importance of physical audits. Even with advanced telemetry systems, occasional manual checks are necessary to ensure accuracy. Human error in data entry or software glitches can occur, and a physical count can serve as a fail-safe. Conduct these audits systematically—perhaps every quarter or bi-annually—to cross-verify your digital records with physical stock.

Communication with your suppliers is also a pivotal element in efficient inventory tracking. Establish a clear line of communication for placing and adjusting orders. Automated reordering systems can be a game-changer, triggering restock orders when inventory falls below a predefined level. This way, you avoid the pitfalls of last-minute orders, backorders, and potential stockouts. Always try to maintain good relationships with multiple suppliers to ensure a steady supply chain, particularly for popular and high-margin items.

Consistent and accurate inventory tracking also helps in financial forecasting. By understanding your inventory turnover ratio, you can plan for bulk purchases and negotiate better terms with suppliers. The data from your tracking systems can feed into your financial models, helping to refine your cash flow projections and budget allocations. Leveraging this data can help you to scale your business strategically.

Let's talk about tracking specific product categories. Different products sell at different rates, and some may have a shorter shelf life than others. For example, fresh sandwiches and perishables need more frequent monitoring compared to canned sodas. Use your inventory system to set different thresholds for reordering various types of products. This ensures that perishable items are not wasted and that long-shelf-life items are always available.

Employee training is another essential component of effective inventory management. Whether you handle stocking duties yourself or employ a team, everyone involved should understand the importance of accurate inventory tracking. Miscommunication and assumptions can lead to discrepancies in stock levels, which in turn can affect your sales and profitability. Regular training sessions can ensure that everyone aligns with the best practices and uses the tracking systems efficiently.

Sustainability and waste reduction are increasingly becoming important in various sectors, including vending. Efficient tracking helps in minimizing waste by ensuring that perishable items are sold within their shelf life, and non-perishable items are rotated effectively. Additionally, adopting sustainable practices such as recycling packaging material and opting for eco-friendly products can resonate well with the growing environmentally-conscious consumer base.

A final note on technology: the rise of artificial intelligence and machine learning offers exciting possibilities for inventory tracking. Predictive analytics can suggest optimal stock levels based on historical data, seasonal trends, and even weather conditions. Imagine a machine that knows to stock more cold beverages on a hot day or more hot beverages during a cold snap. Implementing such advanced technology might require an upfront investment but can offer significant long-term benefits.

Tracking inventory effectively isn't just about keeping your machines stocked. It's about knowing your business's heartbeat and being able to respond to its needs in real-time. Whether you're just starting or you're looking to scale, diligent inventory management can set the foundation for a robust and profitable vending machine business. By harnessing technology, understanding sales cycles, ensuring communication with suppliers, and committing to regular physical audits, you equip your business for sustained success. This systematic approach paves the way for growth, operational efficiency, and ultimately, customer satisfaction.

Restocking Efficiently

When it comes to vending machine operations, restocking efficiently is a cornerstone of maintaining profitability and ensuring customer satisfaction. An efficiently stocked machine not only maximizes sales but also minimizes downtime, reducing the chances of an out-of-stock situation that can turn away potential customers. Let's dive into some crucial strategies for mastering the art of restocking.

First and foremost, understanding your inventory turnover is essential. Every vending machine location will have its own unique demand patterns, and you'll need to keep a close eye on which products are selling quickly and which are lagging. Utilize inventory management software to track sales data in real-time. This software can provide you with valuable insights, helping you restock high-demand items more frequently while scaling back on what's not moving. By using data analytics, you can predict peak times and plan your restocking schedule accordingly.

Efficient restocking begins with maintaining an organized stockroom. Your inventory should be easily accessible and clearly labeled to facilitate quick and accurate restocking runs. Establish a systematic approach to organizing your inventory, grouping similar items together and ensuring that new shipments are rotated properly to prevent older stock from being wasted. Implement a "first in, first out" (FIFO) system to manage perishable goods, ensuring that older items are sold before newer stock is added.

Timing is everything. Schedule your restocking visits during off-peak hours to minimize disruption to your customers and avoid interfering with the foot traffic around your machines. Early mornings or late evenings are often ideal times for this. Additionally, planning your route effectively can save you time and increase your efficiency. Grouping your machines by location and creating a logical restocking route will minimize travel time and maximize your productivity.

Another key aspect of restocking efficiently is maintaining a consistent inventory level. While it's tempting to overstock each machine to reduce the frequency of your visits, this approach can lead to increased waste, especially with perishable items. Striking a balance is crucial. Monitor your sales patterns and adjust your restocking quantities to meet, but not exceed, customer demand. Consider implementing a just-in-time (JIT) inventory system, which ensures that products are restocked in smaller quantities and more frequently, reducing excess inventory and waste.

Automated Wealth

Automation can be a game-changer when it comes to restocking efficiency. Investing in vending machines with built-in inventory tracking systems can provide real-time data on stock levels, alerting you when an item is running low. Some advanced machines even offer remote monitoring capabilities, allowing you to check inventory levels and receive alerts from your smartphone or computer. This technology can revolutionize your restocking process, enabling you to make data-driven decisions and respond quickly to changing demand.

Communication with your suppliers is another critical component. Establishing a strong relationship with your suppliers ensures that you receive timely deliveries and can quickly adjust orders based on your inventory needs. Work with your suppliers to create a consistent delivery schedule, and maintain a list of backup suppliers to mitigate any potential disruptions. Being proactive in your communications can prevent stock shortages and keep your machines running smoothly.

Efficient restocking also involves periodic machine maintenance. While restocking, take the opportunity to perform basic maintenance tasks such as cleaning the machine, checking for any mechanical issues, and ensuring that all payment systems are functioning correctly. Regular upkeep can prevent more significant problems down the line, keeping your machines operational and avoiding costly downtime.

Your restocking staff plays a crucial role in maintaining efficiency. Whether you're handling the restocking yourself or employing a team, thorough training is essential. Ensure that everyone involved understands the importance of accurate inventory tracking, timely restocking, and maintaining a clean and well-organized stockroom. Providing your staff with checklists and standard operating procedures (SOPs) can streamline the restocking process and ensure consistency.

Customer feedback can offer valuable insights into your restocking strategy. Encourage customers to share their preferences and suggestions, and use this information to fine-tune your inventory. If particular items are frequently requested or sell out quickly, consider adjusting your product mix to better meet customer demands. Satisfied customers are more likely to become repeat customers, boosting your overall sales.

Finally, always be prepared for the unexpected. Keep an emergency inventory of your best-selling items, and have a plan in place for handling unforeseen circumstances, such as supplier delays or sudden spikes in demand. By staying flexible and adaptable, you can ensure that your machines are always well-stocked and ready to serve your customers.

In essence, restocking efficiently is a blend of art and science. It requires careful planning, meticulous organization, and a keen eye on customer preferences and sales data. By leveraging technology, maintaining strong supplier relationships, and continuously refining your strategy, you can optimize your restocking process and keep your vending machines running smoothly and profitably. The result? A thriving vending machine business that delivers consistent, passive income and keeps your customers coming back for more.

Chapter 14:
Customer Service and Relations

Excellent customer service and strong relations are vital to the success of your vending machine business. Addressing customer complaints efficiently not only resolves immediate issues but also enhances your brand's reputation. To turn a disgruntled customer into a loyal one, ensure prompt responses and offer solutions that exceed expectations. Building trust and rapport with your customers can be as simple as maintaining clean, well-stocked machines, and consistently providing high-quality products. A happy customer is more likely to return and spread positive word-of-mouth, which can be one of your most powerful marketing tools. Moreover, consider implementing loyalty programs to reward consistent customers, further encouraging repeat business and customer retention. Remember, fostering an excellent customer relationship doesn't just improve sales; it builds a community around your brand, creating advocates who will support your business for years to come.

Handling Customer Complaints

Customer complaints, while not always pleasant, are an inevitable part of running a vending machine business. How you handle these grievances can make a significant difference in your business's reputation and long-term success. When dealt with correctly, complaints can serve as vital feedback that helps you improve your service and products, ultimately driving customer loyalty.

First and foremost, it's crucial to respond to complaints swiftly. The longer customers wait for their issues to be addressed, the more frustrated they'll become. Implement a system for quickly acknowledging receipt of the complaint, even if you can't resolve it immediately. This simple act of acknowledgment can go a long way in soothing a disgruntled customer.

Listening to your customers is equally important. Really listen. Put yourself in their shoes and understand their frustration. Empathy can turn a potential conflict into a constructive conversation. Make sure to train your team to handle complaints with a listening ear and an empathetic attitude.

Once you've listened, it's time to act. Swift action shows that you value your customers' time and are committed to resolving their issues. Whether it's a refund, a product replacement, or just a sincere apology, make sure the solution addresses the problem adequately. Tailor your response to fit the situation, ensuring it meets the customer's expectations.

Documenting complaints is another critical step. Keeping detailed records of the issues customers have faced and how they were resolved allows you to track recurring problems. This data is invaluable; it can help you identify patterns and implement long-term solutions to prevent similar issues in the future.

Train your employees thoroughly. They should be well-versed in your business's complaint resolution process, as well as the appropriate tone and language to use. Role-playing exercises can be particularly effective in preparing your team for real-life scenarios.

Engage with dissatisfied customers respectfully, and consider using a multi-channel approach. Whether through emails, social media, or direct calls, meet your customers where they feel most comfortable discussing their problems. This flexibility not only aids in quick resolution but also demonstrates your commitment to customer satisfaction.

Enhance your machines to limit complaints. Installing technology that makes transactions smooth and adding features like customer support contact details or a direct line to your service team inside the vending machine can preempt many issues. Also, regularly check your machines to ensure they are functioning correctly and stocked adequately.

Utilize feedback surveys. Post-interaction surveys can give customers a platform to voice their concerns and satisfaction levels. This feedback serves as an actionable insight that helps you continuously fine-tune your service better to meet customer expectations.

Transparency is essential. If there's an issue customers should be aware of, such as a machine being out of service for maintenance, inform them proactively. Use signs or digital notifications to keep them updated. Transparency builds trust and can preempt many potential complaints.

An often overlooked yet significant strategy is turning complaints into opportunities. Use the feedback to innovate and improve. For example, if multiple customers complain about a lack of healthy options, introduce a new range of healthier products. This not only resolves the complaint but also enhances your offering.

Emphasize a customer-first mentality in your business culture. When your entire team values customer satisfaction as a top priority, handling complaints becomes an extension of your service, not a separate, burdensome task. Regular training sessions and team meetings focused on customer service can reinforce this principle.

Finally, follow up. After a complaint is resolved, reach out to the customer to ensure they are satisfied with how their issue was handled.

This follow-up conversation can rebuild damaged relationships and show that you genuinely care about their experience.

Handling customer complaints effectively is about more than just solving the immediate problem. It's about demonstrating your commitment to your customers, learning from the feedback, and continuously improving. By adopting these strategies, you'll not only resolve issues efficiently but also build a loyal customer base that sees you as a reliable and customer-centric business.

Building Customer Loyalty

When it comes to running a successful vending machine business, building customer loyalty is crucial. This isn't just about repeat sales; it's about creating an experience that encourages customers to continually come back to your machines. But how do you foster this kind of loyalty, especially in a business often viewed as impersonal? Let's dive into some strategies that can make a big difference.

First off, let's talk about the importance of product variety and quality. Offering a diverse range of products caters to different tastes and dietary preferences, which can make your vending machines more appealing. Stocking healthy snacks alongside traditional favorites, for example, can attract a broader audience. Additionally, ensuring that the products are fresh and of high quality will leave a lasting, positive impression on your customers.

Another effective way to build customer loyalty is through personalization and customer engagement. This may sound challenging in the vending business, but technology makes it easier. Implementing customer feedback mechanisms, such as QR codes that customers can scan to leave reviews or suggest products, can make them feel heard and valued. In turn, this can boost their loyalty to your brand.

Consistency is another key factor in building trust and loyalty with your customers. Make sure your machines are reliable and stocked consistently. Few things frustrate customers more than encountering an empty or malfunctioning machine. Regular maintenance and prompt restocking can mitigate these issues and keep your customers coming back.

Promotions and loyalty programs are also effective tools for enhancing customer retention. You can offer discounts, free products, or even a points-based system where frequent buyers earn rewards. Promotions not only attract new customers but also give existing ones a reason to return regularly.

Customer service can't be overlooked, even in a vending business. Make it easy for customers to report issues and ensure you respond promptly. A simple contact sticker on your machines with a customer service number or email can go a long way. Quick, satisfactory resolutions to issues like jammed products or malfunctioning machines can turn a frustrated customer into a loyal one.

To further humanize your vending business, consider aligning with local events and community activities. Sponsorships or partnerships with local organizations can tie your business more closely to the community, enhancing customer loyalty. People are generally more inclined to support businesses they feel are contributing to their local area.

Loyalty isn't just about maintaining a customer base, it's also about creating brand advocates who will recommend your machines to others. Word-of-mouth is a powerful tool, especially when it comes from happy, loyal customers. Encouraging satisfied customers to share their experiences can organically boost your brand's reputation.

Another key aspect to focus on is transparency. Clear, honest communication can establish trust. Customers appreciate knowing exactly what they're getting and what to expect. This could mean providing transparent pricing and prominently displaying nutritional information for food items.

Additionally, embracing cashless payment options can make a huge difference in customer satisfaction. Today's consumers are increasingly comfortable with and often prefer using digital payment methods. Offering a range of payment options like credit/debit cards, mobile payments, and even cryptocurrency can make transactions smoother and more convenient, increasing the likelihood of repeat business.

Surveys and regular check-ins can be invaluable. They help you understand your customers' evolving needs and preferences. By acting on the feedback you receive, you demonstrate that you value their opinions, which can strengthen their loyalty to your brand. Simple tools like email surveys or in-app feedback forms for tech-savvy vending machines can provide insights without being overly intrusive.

Remember, building customer loyalty is a continuous process. It's about making ongoing improvements and consistently meeting or exceeding expectations. By paying attention to the small details, you show your customers that their satisfaction is your priority, fostering long-term loyalty.

In summary, building customer loyalty in the vending machine business involves a combination of quality products, excellent customer service, reliability, and engagement. Promotional strategies, community involvement, and embracing technology are also crucial. By focusing on these areas, you can create a loyal customer base that will not only continue to use your vending machines but also recommend them to others.

Ultimately, a loyal customer base is one of the most valuable assets for your vending business. It not only helps stabilize your income but also opens doors for growth and expansion. Happy, loyal customers are likely to spend more, recommend your services, and provide valuable feedback for continuous improvement. In this competitive industry, those who prioritize customer loyalty can gain a significant advantage, ensuring long-term success and profitability.

Building this loyalty isn't an overnight task—it requires strategic planning, consistent execution, and a customer-focused mindset. So, keep your customers at the heart of your business, and you'll see the rewards in their loyalty and your bottom line.

Chapter 15: Technology and Innovations

Technology is rapidly transforming the vending machine industry, enabling entrepreneurs to push the boundaries of efficiency and customer satisfaction. Leveraging advanced vending software allows operators to monitor inventory, track sales, and even gauge customer preferences in real-time—a game-changer for scaling quickly and intelligently. Integrating cashless payment systems is no longer optional but essential; it opens doors to a broader customer base by accommodating various payment methods, from credit cards to mobile wallets. These technological advancements foster convenience and reliability, enhancing both user experience and operational efficiency. By embracing these innovations, you not only stay ahead of the curve but also invigorate your business model, making it resilient and adaptable to future trends.

Utilizing Vending Software

In today's rapidly evolving business landscape, technology plays a pivotal role in driving efficiency and maximizing profitability. For aspiring entrepreneurs and seasoned business owners eyeing the vending machine industry, mastering the art of "Utilizing Vending Software" can serve as a game-changer. This section is designed to shed light on how to harness software solutions to streamline operations, reduce costs, and enhance customer satisfaction.

To start, let's address why vending software is critical. Gone are the days when managing vending machines meant manually checking stock levels and wrestling with mechanical failures. Vending software allows you to oversee your entire fleet of machines from a centralized dashboard. This isn't about just saving time; it's about making smarter business decisions. Imagine being able to see which products are your best sellers across multiple locations, or receiving an alert when a machine is running low on inventory—without having to leave your office. Vending software eliminates guesswork, giving you data at your fingertips.

One of the primary features of modern vending software is real-time inventory management. This capability not only helps in ensuring that your machines are always stocked with popular items but also assists in maintaining a balanced inventory. Why does this matter? Because an empty or poorly stocked machine is a lost opportunity for sales. By tracking stock levels in real-time, you can set reorder points and automate the replenishment process. The software can even help predict future sales trends based on historical data, allowing for more accurate inventory planning and minimizing waste.

Beyond inventory, another crucial aspect is remote monitoring and diagnostics. Remember the days when a broken machine meant lost revenue until someone could come and fix it? With advanced vending software, you get immediate alerts about any issues, be it a jammed slot or a payment system failure. The real charm lies in the preventative maintenance features. Many software platforms can diagnose potential problems before they become significant issues, guiding maintenance personnel on what needs to be addressed before a breakdown halts operations. These predictive insights can significantly reduce downtime and repair costs.

Now, let's talk about data analytics. It's one thing to have data; it's another to use it effectively. Vending software can generate various reports that provide insights into your sales performance, customer preferences, and machine efficiency. For instance, you might find that gum sells faster in office buildings, while energy drinks are more popular in gyms. Such detailed reporting allows you to customize product offerings and optimize locations for maximum profitability. Additionally, you can track the performance of different machines and identify which ones are underperforming, laying the groundwork for data-driven decisions regarding machine placement or replacement.

What about customer satisfaction? That's where customer interaction interfaces in vending software come into play. Some advanced systems offer features like cashless payment options and mobile app integrations, making it easier and more convenient for customers to make purchases. These features don't just meet modern consumer expectations but exceed them, providing a seamless user experience that can bolster customer loyalty. For businesses looking to target tech-savvy consumers, offering mobile payments or QR code-based promotions can give a competitive edge.

One often overlooked benefit of utilizing vending software is its role in compliance and reporting. From health and safety regulations to financial auditing, digital records simplify compliance. You can keep track of all transactions and ensure that your business adheres to required standards without the hassle of manual record-keeping. Automated reporting can save hours of administrative work and provide peace of mind knowing that you can easily generate the necessary documents for any audits or inspections.

Furthermore, vending software can be an invaluable tool for marketing and promotions. Built-in features often include options for running promotions, discounts, and loyalty programs directly through the machines. For instance, you could offer a discount for customers who use a particular payment method or create a loyalty program where frequent buyers earn points redeemable for free products. These marketing tactics are not just about boosting sales but also about building a relationship with your customers. Software solutions can track the success of these promotions, helping you refine strategies for better results.

An interesting feature that is gaining traction is the use of artificial intelligence and machine learning within vending software. These cutting-edge technologies can analyze customer behavior, predict trends, and even optimize machine placement based on complex algorithms. Imagine a system that knows what products to stock during different times of the year, or one that suggests the best locations for new machines based on demographic data. AI and machine learning are pushing the boundaries of what's possible in the vending industry, turning data into actionable insights and facilitating smarter business decisions.

Security is another crucial aspect managed by vending software. As these systems often handle transactions, they come with built-in security features to protect against fraud and data breaches. Whether it's encryption of customer payment details or secure cloud-based storage of business data, the right software ensures that all sensitive information is well-protected. This not only instills confidence among your customers but also shields your business from potential risks associated with data theft.

Finally, let's consider the integration capabilities of vending software. The most effective solutions can integrate seamlessly with other business tools you might be using, such as accounting software, CRM systems, or even supplier management platforms. This interconnectedness allows for a unified approach to managing your vending operations, where data flows seamlessly from one tool to another. For example, sales data from your vending software can automatically update your accounting records, helping maintain accurate financial statements without manual entries.

In summary, utilizing vending software is about harnessing the power of technology to gain a competitive edge in the vending machine business. From real-time inventory management to predictive maintenance, and from detailed analytics to enhanced customer experiences, these systems offer a multitude of benefits. As you venture into or expand your vending machine enterprise, investing in the right software can provide the tools needed to drive efficiency and profitability. Embrace the digital transformation, and you will find yourself well-equipped to tackle the challenges of modern vending business operations.

Integrating Cashless Payment Systems

As we cruise further into the twenty-first century, technology continues to revolutionize the vending machine industry, making it more efficient, customer-friendly, and potentially more profitable. One of the most significant advancements in recent years is the integration of cashless payment systems. This move towards cashless transactions not only aligns with the increasing adoption of digital payment methods worldwide but also opens up numerous advantages for your vending machine business.

For starters, consider the sheer convenience offered by cashless payment options. Customers no longer need to fumble with coins or worry about carrying cash. A quick tap or scan and they're done. This ease of use can significantly reduce barriers to purchase, thereby increasing your sales volume. In an era where everyone from teenagers to senior citizens are familiar with digital payments, integrating cashless options ensures you cater to a broader audience.

But the benefits extend beyond just convenience for your customers. Cashless payment systems can tremendously simplify your operations. They reduce the need for manual cash collection, counting, and banking, which can be both time-consuming and prone to errors. Instead, you get real-time financial data, allowing you to track your sales accurately and gauge the performance of different machines and products. This detailed data can provide critical insights for refining your product mix, optimizing placements, and even setting promotional strategies.

Moreover, cashless systems generally offer enhanced security features. Cash is inherently risky—prone to theft, loss, or vandalism. By minimizing cash handling, you can mitigate these risks, giving you peace of mind and potentially reducing your insurance premiums. Most cashless systems come with robust encryption standards and fraud detection mechanisms, further ensuring the safety of your financial transactions.

Another often overlooked benefit is the potential to gather valuable customer data. Cashless payment systems can be integrated with CRM (Customer Relationship Management) tools, providing insights into customer buying habits and preferences. For example, you can track repeat customers, identify peak shopping times, and monitor the performance of specific products. Armed with this information, you can tailor your marketing campaigns, stock up on popular products, and even offer personalized promotions, all of which can drive customer loyalty and increased sales.

When it comes to choosing a cashless payment system, the options are varied. Broadly, you can categorize them into a few major types: NFC (Near-Field Communication) payments, card readers, and mobile payment apps. NFC-enabled systems allow customers to simply tap their contactless cards or smartphones on a reader. This is incredibly fast and convenient. Card readers, which accept both debit and credit cards, offer another versatile option. Mobile payment apps like Apple Pay, Google Wallet, and even some cryptocurrency wallets provide additional flexibility, appealing especially to younger, tech-savvy customers.

Let's take a closer look at the installation process. Integrating a cashless system into your existing vending machines is generally straightforward but varies depending on the machine's make and model. Modern vending machines often come with built-in options or easy-to-install kits for adding cashless functionality. For older models, retrofitting might be necessary. First, you'll likely need to consult your machine's manufacturer or a specialized technician to ensure compatibility. Next, purchase the required hardware, which usually includes a card reader, a communication system, and possibly an external antenna for enhancing signal reception.

Once the hardware is in place, the software integration is the next step. Most cashless systems come with user-friendly software that can be installed either directly on the machine or through a centralized management system. Ensure your software is up-to-date to support the latest security protocols and features. Conduct thorough testing to ensure all systems are working seamlessly, and don't forget to train your staff on using and troubleshooting the new system.

Of course, integrating cashless payment systems involves an upfront investment. The cost of hardware, installation, and potential upgrades can add up. However, consider it as a long-term investment. The efficiencies it brings—be it in operations, security, or customer satisfaction—often pay for themselves over time. Furthermore, many cashless system providers offer flexible payment plans or leasing options to ease the financial burden. It's also worth exploring partnerships or incentives from financial institutions that may offer discounts or promotional deals for adopting digital payment solutions.

On the marketing front, don't forget to highlight your cashless capabilities. Signage on the machines and marketing materials can be essential to inform customers that they can pay using their preferred digital methods. You can even run promotional campaigns, offering small discounts or rewards for using cashless payments. This not only encourages usage but also makes your vending machines more modern and appealing.

In the grand scheme, as you continue to grow your vending machine business, staying up-to-date with technological innovations like cashless payment systems isn't just a nice-to-have—it's a necessity. As the world continues to shift towards digital transactions, failing to integrate cashless payment systems could mean losing out on a significant segment of your potential customer base. Conversely, early adopters often gain a competitive edge, attracting tech-savvy consumers and enhancing their brand's reputation.

In wrapping up, integrating cashless payment systems offers a multitude of benefits—from boosting convenience and operational efficiency to enhancing security and providing invaluable customer insights. While it requires an initial investment and careful planning, the long-term payoff in customer satisfaction, operational simplicity, and increased sales makes it a compelling addition to your vending machine business strategy. So take the plunge. Embrace the future of vending, and watch your business flourish.

Chapter 16: Automating Your Business

Streamlining your vending machine business with automation is not just a convenience—it's a game-changer. Leveraging advanced tools and technology can free up precious time, reduce human error, and ultimately increase your profitability. Consider integrating inventory management software that monitors stock levels in real-time and sends automatic restock alerts. Embracing remote monitoring systems allows you to manage machines from anywhere, minimizing downtime and enhancing customer satisfaction. Automation can also extend to cashless payment options, which not only attract more customers but also simplify financial tracking. By reducing manual labor through these innovative solutions, you can focus your efforts on scaling your operations and exploring new business opportunities. Automation isn't just a trend; it's the future of the vending machine industry, ensuring your business remains competitive and efficient in an ever-evolving market.

Leveraging Automation Tools

Automation tools are no longer just a luxury for large corporations; they're a necessity for businesses of all sizes, including vending machine operations. As an aspiring entrepreneur or existing business owner aiming to create a sustainable and profitable passive income stream, leveraging automation tools can be a game-changer. From simplifying daily operations to providing valuable insights into customer behavior, these tools can significantly streamline your workflow, reduce manual labor, and, most importantly, help you focus on scaling your business rather than getting bogged down by mundane tasks.

First off, let's talk about inventory management. One of the most labor-intensive aspects of running a vending machine business is keeping track of inventory. Manual tracking not only consumes time but is also prone to human error. Automation tools can eliminate these issues by providing real-time inventory updates. These systems can notify you when stock levels fall below a certain threshold, thereby ensuring that your machines are always well-stocked. Some advanced tools even integrate with your suppliers, allowing for automatic reorders. This seamless process reduces the risk of stockouts and ensures that your customers always find what they're looking for, enhancing their satisfaction and loyalty.

Next on the list is predictive analytics. By analyzing past sales data, these tools can forecast future trends, helping you to make more informed decisions about which products to stock and in what quantities. Predictive analytics can identify patterns such as peak sales times, customer preferences, and even seasonal demand changes. This data-driven approach allows you to optimize your inventory and meet customer demand efficiently, potentially increasing your sales and profits. Moreover, these insights can guide you in making strategic decisions about expanding your product range or introducing new offerings, thereby keeping your business relevant and competitive.

Now, let's delve into route optimization. For vending machine operators managing multiple locations, planning the most efficient routes for restocking and maintenance can be daunting. Route optimization tools use algorithms to determine the quickest and most efficient paths, saving time and reducing fuel costs. These tools can also factor in real-time traffic conditions, ensuring that your staff spends less time on the road and more time servicing machines. By improving the efficiency of your operations, you can attend to more machines in less time, thereby increasing overall productivity.

An equally vital aspect of automation is customer relationship management (CRM). Modern CRM tools allow you to capture and analyze customer feedback systematically. Whether through direct interactions, social media comments, or online reviews, these tools compile customer insights into actionable data. You can then use this information to improve service quality, address issues proactively, and even personalize marketing campaigns. A well-implemented CRM system can enhance customer satisfaction and loyalty, which are crucial for the long-term success of your vending machine business.

Consider the power of automated financial management tools. Manually tracking expenses, revenues, and profits can be cumbersome and error-prone. Automation tools can link directly to your transactions, categorizing income and expenses automatically. This makes it easier to track your financial health, identify trends, and make informed budgeting decisions. Automated invoicing and payment systems can also speed up your cash flow, ensuring that you get paid faster. Efficient financial management is key to sustaining and growing your business, and automation can make this much less of a headache.

Another area where automation can make a significant impact is in marketing. Tools like email marketing platforms can automate your communication with customers, sending personalized emails based on customer behavior and preferences. Social media automation tools can schedule posts, manage interactions, and analyze the performance of your social media campaigns. These tools can help you maintain a consistent online presence with minimal effort, attracting and retaining customers. Moreover, data from these campaigns can provide insights into what works and what doesn't, enabling you to fine-tune your marketing strategies for better results.

Automated Wealth

Additionally, consider the value of automated maintenance alerts. Vending machines, like any other mechanical devices, require regular upkeep to function optimally. Automated maintenance tools can monitor machine performance in real-time, alerting you to potential issues before they escalate into significant problems. This proactive approach not only ensures that your machines are always in good working condition but also reduces downtime, which can translate to lost revenue. Some advanced systems even offer predictive maintenance, using data analytics to foresee potential issues and address them proactively.

Security can also benefit from automation. Automated surveillance systems can monitor your vending machines round-the-clock, alerting you to unauthorized access or vandalism. Some systems even come with features like facial recognition and remote monitoring, allowing you to ensure your machines' safety from anywhere. This can be particularly advantageous for machines located in remote or less secure areas. Enhanced security not only protects your assets but also gives customers peace of mind, making them more likely to trust and use your machines.

One can't overlook the significance of integrating cashless payment systems. With the increasing shift towards digital payments, equipping your vending machines with cashless payment options is almost a necessity. Automated payment systems can accept various forms of digital payments, from credit cards to mobile wallets, making transactions quick and convenient for customers. These systems can also provide real-time payment data, helping you better understand sales patterns and customer preferences. Moreover, cashless systems reduce the need for manual cash handling, minimizing the risks of theft and human error.

Finally, centralizing all these automated tools into a comprehensive vending management system can bring immeasurable benefits. Such systems allow you to control various aspects of your business from a single platform, providing a holistic view of your operations. You can monitor sales, track inventory, manage routes, oversee payments, and even analyze customer behavior from one place. This centralized approach simplifies management, reduces the need for multiple software solutions, and enhances decision-making capabilities. In the long run, having an integrated system can save you time, reduce costs, and significantly improve your business's efficiency and profitability.

While the initial investment in automation tools might seem steep, the long-term benefits they offer far outweigh the costs. By reducing manual labor, minimizing errors, and optimizing various aspects of your operations, these tools can help you run a leaner, more efficient business. They free up your time, allowing you to focus on strategic planning and expansion rather than getting mired in day-to-day operations. In an industry as competitive as vending machines, leveraging automation can give you a significant edge, positioning your business for sustained success and growth.

In sum, leveraging automation tools isn't just about keeping up with the times; it's about staying ahead of the curve. As you embark on or continue your journey in the vending machine business, investing in these tools can pave the way for more streamlined operations, improved customer satisfaction, and ultimately, higher profitability. By embracing automation, you're not just making your life easier; you're setting your business up for a future of sustained growth and success.

Reducing Manual Labor

Running a successful vending machine business can be an incredibly lucrative endeavor, but it can also be labor-intensive if not managed efficiently. Reducing manual labor is a key strategy for maximizing profitability and freeing up time to focus on growing your business.

Automation plays a crucial role in streamlining operations and minimizing the need for hands-on involvement.

One of the first steps to reducing manual labor involves leveraging technology. Modern vending machines offer advanced features such as remote monitoring, which allows you to keep track of inventory levels, machine performance, and financial transactions in real time from a centralized dashboard. These systems not only save time but also provide valuable insights that can help you make informed business decisions. For example, you can quickly identify which products are selling well and which are not, enabling you to adjust your inventory accordingly.

Remote monitoring also means fewer trips to each vending machine. Rather than visiting each location to check stock levels or troubleshoot issues, you can assess the situation from your computer or smartphone. When you do need to restock or perform maintenance, you can plan your route more efficiently, focusing on machines that need immediate attention. This targeted approach reduces travel time and fuel costs, adding to your overall savings.

Another way to reduce manual labor is by utilizing vending management software (VMS). VMS solutions integrate various aspects of your business operations, from sales tracking to route planning. These platforms can automate tasks that would otherwise require significant time and effort. For instance, some VMS can generate reports on sales trends, helping you to forecast demand and plan inventory purchases more accurately. Moreover, automated alerts can notify you of issues such as low stock or mechanical failures, allowing you to address problems promptly before they impact your revenue.

Let's not forget about the actual machines themselves. Investing in high-quality, reliable vending machines can significantly cut down on maintenance requirements. Look for machines that offer self-diagnostic features. These machines can identify and sometimes even resolve issues without human intervention. In cases where manual action is required, the machine provides a clear diagnostic report, pinpointing the problem and reducing the time needed for repairs.

An often-overlooked aspect of reducing manual labor is the method of payment accepted by your vending machines. Traditional machines that only accept cash require regular collection and manual counting of money, which is both time-consuming and prone to errors. By integrating cashless payment systems, you can not only offer convenience to your customers but also streamline your financial management processes. Transactions made via credit card, mobile payment apps, or contactless payment methods are automatically recorded and processed, reducing the need for manual reconciliation.

Automation extends beyond the vending machines themselves. The administrative tasks of managing your business can also benefit from automation. For example, accounting software can automate invoicing, payroll, and expense tracking. Many solutions offer integration with your vending management software, creating a seamless flow of data that eliminates duplicate entries and minimizes human error. By automating these back-office functions, you can free up valuable time to focus on strategic planning and business development.

Inventory management is another critical area where automation can make a difference. Implementing barcode scanning or RFID technology in your storage facilities can expedite the process of tracking inventory levels and movements. Automated systems can notify you when stock is running low and even generate purchase orders for replenishment. This eliminates the need for manual counting and reduces the risk of stockouts, ensuring your machines are always well-stocked and operational.

Additionally, employing third-party logistics providers for restocking can further reduce the manual workload. These companies specialize in inventory management and can handle the entire restocking process for you. By outsourcing this task, you can leverage their expertise and infrastructure, ensuring that your machines are always stocked efficiently and accurately. This approach also allows you to scale your business more easily, as adding new machines or locations doesn't result in a proportional increase in manual labor.

Staffing is another area where automation and strategic planning can help reduce manual labor. While human oversight and interaction are necessary, particularly for quality control and customer service, many routine tasks can be automated or outsourced. For example, customer inquiries and complaints can be managed through automated ticketing systems or chatbots, providing timely resolutions without requiring constant human intervention. This ensures that essential customer service functions are maintained while reducing the workload on your team.

Finally, an essential element of reducing manual labor is continuous improvement. Regularly evaluating your processes and seeking out new technologies or methods to streamline operations can lead to incremental reductions in manual labor over time. Encourage your team to provide feedback on current processes and suggest areas for improvement. Often, those who are performing the tasks day-to-day have valuable insights into inefficiencies and potential solutions.

In summary, reducing manual labor in your vending machine business isn't just about cutting costs—it's about optimizing every facet of your operations to run as smoothly and efficiently as possible. By leveraging technology, high-quality equipment, and smart systems, you can not only save time but also increase profitability. This allows you to focus on scaling your business and continuing to provide excellent service to your customers.

Embrace the power of automation and let your business work for you, transforming what might seem like a labor-intensive endeavor into a streamlined, efficient, and highly profitable operation.

Chapter 17: Expanding Your Business

When you've successfully managed your vending machine operations and identified growth opportunities, it's time to think about expansion. Scaling your business involves more than just adding more machines; it requires strategic planning and thoughtful execution. Begin by assessing your current business model and identifying which aspects are scalable. Consider exploring new markets or upgrading to state-of-the-art machines that offer healthier options or advanced payment systems. An essential strategy could be franchising your model, allowing you to expand rapidly without stretching your resources thin. Network with industry professionals to gain insights and stay current with market trends, ensuring your expansion aligns with consumer demands. Remember, growth is not just about increasing the number of machines but also enhancing your brand's reach and operational efficiency.

Scaling Strategies

Expanding your vending machine business doesn't just mean buying more machines. It's a multifaceted endeavor requiring strategic planning, resource allocation, and a clear vision of your long-term goals. Scaling up involves understanding both the opportunities and challenges that come with growth. Are you ready to take your business to the next level? Let's dive into the strategies that can make scaling both manageable and effective.

Automated Wealth

First, let's talk about capital investment. Scaling usually needs financial input, whether you're investing in new machines, expanding to new locations, or enhancing your logistics. Before making any financial commitments, ensure your current operations are profitable. Evaluate your cash flow and consider different financing options. For some, reinvesting profits is a viable path, but others may explore small business loans or investor funding. Each route has its benefits and risks, so choose wisely.

Next, assess your current operations' efficiency. Growth might magnify any existing inefficiencies. Routine operations like restocking and maintenance should run smoothly before you consider scaling up. Are you losing time and money due to outdated practices? Perhaps it's time to streamline these processes by implementing advanced vending management software that can automate inventory tracking and maintenance schedules. Automation could be a game-changer, freeing up time and resources that you can direct toward growth.

Location, location, location! Just as it was when you first started, identifying high-traffic locations is crucial when you're looking to scale. Conduct thorough market research to identify potential new locations. Consider demographics, foot traffic, and proximity to your competition. Negotiate favorable terms with property owners, and don't shy away from diversifying your locations—think schools, office buildings, and even gyms. A well-distributed network of machines can capture diverse revenue streams.

Don't underestimate the power of brand recognition. As you scale, maintaining consistency in your branding becomes increasingly important. Your brand should be recognizable whether it's on a machine located in a hospital or a corporate office. Consistent branding includes everything from your logo and colors to the quality of products you offer. Customers should receive the same level of service no matter where they encounter your vending machines. Consistent experiences build trust, and trust translates to repeat business.

One crucial step is diversifying your product offerings. While it's easy to stick with what has worked so far, growth offers the perfect opportunity to pilot new products. Healthy snacks, specialized beverages, or even tech gadgets can provide fresh revenue streams. Keep an eye on market trends and customer preferences to fine-tune your product mix. You might even consider seasonal variations to capitalize on current trends—think hot beverages in the winter months and cold, refreshing treats in the summer.

Partnerships and collaborations can provide unexpected avenues for growth. Aligning with other businesses can offer mutual benefits. For instance, partnering with local food producers can not only differentiate your product line but also support other local businesses. Consider forming alliances with gyms, schools, or offices to create exclusive vending agreements that guarantee you a customer base while providing them with tailored offerings.

Hiring and training staff becomes more pertinent as you scale. More machines mean more maintenance, more inventory to manage, and, inevitably, more customer interactions. Ensuring your team is well-trained and motivated can be a significant competitive advantage. Offer training sessions that focus on customer service, technical troubleshooting, and efficient inventory management. Happy employees usually lead to satisfied customers, boosting your overall business performance.

Financial management becomes increasingly complex as your business grows. Implement a robust accounting system that can handle multiple revenue streams and various expenses. Consistently review your financial statements and adapt your strategies based on these insights. Effective financial planning can mean the difference between sustained growth and unexpected pitfalls. Moreover, maintaining a flexible budget allows you to seize new opportunities or weather economic downturns without jeopardizing your business.

A customer relationship management (CRM) system can offer significant advantages during scaling. Keeping track of customer preferences, feedback, and purchasing patterns can help you tailor your services more effectively. Personalized experiences can significantly impact customer loyalty and satisfaction. Sending out periodic surveys or feedback forms can provide invaluable insights into what you are doing right and areas that need improvement.

Another powerful strategy lies in leveraging technology. As you expand, consider integrating more advanced technologies like AI for predictive maintenance and analytics for data-driven decision-making. Technologies such as contactless payments and mobile app integrations can enhance user experience and attract a tech-savvy clientele. These advancements can improve operational efficiency and provide a competitive edge.

Scaling also involves navigating legal considerations. As you expand into new geographical areas, you'll need to comply with local laws and regulations, which may differ from your current operating locations. This can include new licensing requirements, health and safety regulations, or even environmental considerations. Ensuring compliance across all operational areas can prevent potential legal challenges that could hinder your growth.

Networking can be an underutilized tool. Building relationships within the vending machine industry can provide opportunities for mentorship, collaboration, and staying updated with industry trends. Attending industry conferences and workshops can open doors to new partnerships and innovative ideas that can fuel your growth. Don't underestimate the value of learning from others' experiences and leveraging collective industry wisdom.

Lastly, always keep an eye on sustainability and eco-friendly practices. Modern consumers are increasingly environmentally conscious, and a commitment to sustainability can set your business apart. Consider investing in energy-efficient machines, using biodegradable packaging, and offering eco-friendly products. Not only can these actions reduce your environmental footprint, but they also resonate well with a growing segment of the market.

Scaling your vending machine business is a multifaceted challenge, but with the right strategies, it can be a rewarding journey. Every decision should be informed and aligned with your long-term goals. By focusing on efficiency, diversification, technology, and maintaining strong relationships, you can successfully navigate the complexities of growth and drive your business to new heights.

Considering Franchising

You're standing at the crossroads of growth with your vending machine business, wondering whether franchising could be the gateway to exponential success. Franchising provides a dual benefit: it allows you to expand your business footprint while empowering other aspiring entrepreneurs to step into the world of vending machines. Let's examine the various facets of franchising and demystify its potential for transforming your enterprise.

First, let's address the fundamental question: what exactly is franchising? In simple terms, franchising is a partnership between two parties— the franchisor (you) and the franchisee (the person who buys the right to operate a business unit using your trademark, systems, and support). By franchising your vending machine business, you're essentially licensing out your proven business model for others to replicate, in exchange for initial and ongoing fees.

Why consider franchising in the first place? The answer lies in scalability. Franchising offers an efficient way to scale your business without bearing the full burden of capital expenditure or the day-to-day operational hassles. It's a symbiotic relationship. The franchisee handles local operations and investments, while you provide a robust blueprint, training, and ongoing support. This partnership enables faster market penetration and potentially greater profitability than you might achieve solo.

Imagine this: your brand's vending machines installed in different cities, offering a uniform standard of quality and service. The beauty of this model is that each franchisee has a vested interest in seeing their franchise succeed. Their investment of both time and money acts as a powerful motivator, ensuring higher levels of commitment and performance.

However, the road to franchising isn't devoid of challenges. One major hurdle is ensuring consistency across multiple franchise locations. As appealing as the concept might be, it demands rigorous standardization of your vending business operations. From software and hardware to product sourcing and customer service, every aspect needs to be meticulously documented and standardized. This will ensure the franchisees align with your brand's vision and operational efficiency.

Now, let's discuss the essential steps to get started with franchising:

- **Create a Comprehensive Franchising Model:** Your first step is to develop a detailed franchising plan. This includes crafting a franchise agreement and a franchise disclosure document (FDD). These documents spell out all the details—rights, obligations, fees, training procedures, marketing support, and operational guidelines.

- **Set Up a Training Program:** To ensure the uniformity of service and quality, you'll need to create a robust training program. This program should cover everything from operating the vending machines to customer service and inventory management.

- **Develop Marketing and Sales Support:** Provide franchisees with marketing materials and strategies to attract customers in their local regions. This support can range from digital marketing strategies to in-store promotions and customer loyalty programs.

- **Legal Compliance:** Ensure all your franchising efforts comply with federal and state regulations. Consulting with a legal expert specializing in franchising is highly recommended to avoid any legal pitfalls.

An often overlooked but crucial aspect of franchising is selecting the right franchisees. Selling a franchise isn't just about finding someone willing to pay the fees. Look for individuals who share your passion for the vending machine business, have a solid business acumen, and ideally, possess some experience in the retail or service industry. Their dedication and capabilities will significantly impact the success of their franchise, and by extension, your overall brand reputation.

It's also worth mentioning the importance of location even in the franchising model. Guide your franchisees on how to select high-traffic areas and negotiate agreements with property owners. The profitability of their franchise will rely heavily on its strategic placement, something you've hopefully mastered in your own business journey.

As your network of franchisees grows, so does the complexity of managing and supporting them. Invest in technology solutions that facilitate efficient communication, monitoring, and support. Whether it's customer relationship management (CRM) systems or specialized vending machine software, modern tools can help maintain smooth operations and timely troubleshooting.

Automated Wealth

While the prospects of franchising are undeniably compelling, it's equally important to acknowledge the financial aspects. Initial franchising setup costs can be substantial, covering legal fees, consultant fees, marketing expenses, and the development of training programs. The revenue model typically includes an initial franchise fee followed by ongoing royalties based on a percentage of each franchisee's revenue. Conduct a detailed financial analysis to ensure that these fees are structured in a way that's both profitable for you and fair to the franchisee.

Franchising also opens doors for more diversified revenue streams. Beyond franchise fees and royalties, you can generate income through product sales to franchisees, service agreements, and even mentoring programs. These additional revenue channels can provide financial stability and an impetus for further innovation.

At its core, franchising is about building a community. A successful franchise network thrives on robust relationships between the franchisor and franchisees. Regular meetings, workshops, and a transparent communication channel can foster trust and collective growth. Celebrate the successes of your franchisees, offer awards and recognitions, and create a culture of continuous improvement. When franchisees feel valued and supported, their motivation and business performance naturally amplify.

Envision your brand as a lighthouse guiding numerous captains steering their own ships. Each franchisee, though sailing their own route, looks up to the lighthouse for direction and assurance. Your role as a franchisor extends beyond the initial sale; it's about steering this collective fleet towards mutual prosperity.

In conclusion, while considering franchising, it's essential to weigh both the opportunities and challenges. Franchising offers a pathway to expand your vending machine empire with less direct capital investment and operational control—as long as you maintain rigorous standards and provide unwavering support. It's a journey requiring meticulous planning, robust training, and strategic partnerships. When done right, franchising can transform your business into a far-reaching brand, impacting communities and fostering entrepreneurial spirit in others. The decision to franchise should be anchored in your long-term vision, ambition, and readiness to extend your leadership to a wider network.

CHAPTER 18: EVALUATING YOUR SUCCESS

Taking the time to evaluate your success is crucial in the vending machine business. You need to regularly review key performance indicators (KPIs) like machine uptime, sales metrics, and customer feedback to gauge the overall health of your venture. Conducting thorough, periodic reviews allows you to pinpoint what's working and what's not, enabling you to make data-driven decisions that can propel your business forward. Whether it's analyzing the profitability of specific locations or assessing the effectiveness of your marketing strategies, understanding these metrics will help you optimize and grow. Remember, the ultimate goal is to create a sustainable and profitable operation, so keep refining your approach based on your evaluations.

Key Performance Indicators

Evaluating your success in the vending machine business isn't just about counting how many machines you have out in the field or the dollar signs flashing in your financial statements. One of the most actionable ways to measure your performance is through Key Performance Indicators (KPIs). By drilling down into these metrics, you can identify what's working, what needs improvement, and where to focus your energy for optimal growth.

The most fundamental KPI in the vending machine business is sales revenue. This is the total dollar amount generated by your machines over a given period. However, simply tracking revenue can be misleading if you don't account for costs. Therefore, it's prudent to also measure profit margins. Profit margin is calculated by subtracting the total cost of goods sold (COGS) from your total revenue and then dividing that number by total revenue. This tells you how much profit you're making for every dollar of sales, giving you a clearer picture of financial health.

Another critical KPI is machine uptime. This measures the percentage of time your machines are operational and dispensing products. Downtime means lost revenue, so maintaining high uptime is essential for success. Regular maintenance routines can help keep this percentage high. Consider adopting a proactive maintenance schedule rather than a reactive one, which means addressing potential issues before they become actual problems.

Inventory turnover ratio is another KPI that should not be overlooked. This ratio measures how often your inventory is sold and replaced over a period. A high turnover rate implies strong sales and efficient inventory management. Conversely, a low turnover rate may suggest that products are not appealing to customers or that inventory management practices need refining. To improve turnover, continually analyze sales data to adjust product offerings to match customer demand better.

Location performance is crucial too. Not all vending machine locations are created equal; some will perform better than others. By measuring the sales performance on a per-location basis, you can identify high-performing locations that may be worth investing more into, or low-performing ones that may need to be reconsidered or relocated. Balancing this KPI with the cost of rent or location fees can help maximize profitability.

Customer satisfaction is another key metric that should resonate deeply with your business strategy. Collect feedback through various channels, such as QR codes on your machines directing customers to a feedback form. High customer satisfaction often correlates with higher sales and repeat business. This metric can be measured through survey results, customer complaints, and social media reviews. Addressing and adapting to customer feedback is vital for long-term success.

Average transaction value (ATV) is yet another KPI worth tracking. This metric measures the average amount spent by a customer per transaction. Increasing ATV can be a sign that customers find your product offerings valuable. Strategies to boost this metric include upselling higher-margin products or offering discounts on bundled items. The better you entice customers to spend more per transaction, the healthier your bottom line will be.

Cash flow is the lifeblood of any business, and the vending machine business is no exception. Monitoring your cash flow metrics, such as the current cash on hand versus liabilities, ensures you can manage operating costs and reinvest in the business. Poor cash flow management can lead to lapses in operations, like running out of products or failing to service machines regularly. Consider leveraging financial software tailored for vending businesses to keep this metric in check.

Expanding on cash flow, the return on investment (ROI) of your machines is an essential KPI that combines both revenue and cost aspects. Calculate ROI by dividing the net profit generated by a machine by the cost of that machine. This KPI tells you how long it will take for each machine to pay for itself and begin generating pure profit. Machines with lower ROI may need closer scrutiny or could be replaced with more efficient models.

The frequency of restocking is a logistical KPI that plays a significant role in operational efficiency. Knowing how often each machine needs to be restocked can help optimize your supply chain and reduce transportation costs. Route planning software can greatly assist in making your restocking process more efficient, saving you time and money while ensuring machines are always fully stocked.

Marketing performance metrics are also indispensable. Track KPIs such as customer acquisition cost (CAC) and customer retention rate (CRR). CAC is the cost of acquiring a new customer, while CRR measures the percentage of customers who continue to make purchases over time. Lowering CAC while maintaining or increasing CRR can provide a substantial boost to profitability. Utilize both online and offline marketing strategies tailored to your target demographics to optimize these metrics.

Employee performance KPIs are just as crucial, particularly as your business scales. Track metrics like employee productivity, the efficiency of tasks completed, and employee satisfaction. Happy and productive employees are more likely to contribute positively to your business, from restocking machines to maintaining customer relationships. Regular training and employee engagement initiatives can further elevate these KPIs.

It's not just about numbers; qualitative metrics can provide insightful perspectives. Conducting periodic reviews that incorporate both quantitative KPIs and qualitative feedback from customers and employees can offer a comprehensive evaluation of your business performance. Combining the hard data with real-world feedback ensures a more well-rounded and actionable assessment.

Lastly, consider implementing a balanced scorecard approach to view multiple KPIs in tandem. This methodology allows you to align your business activities to the vision and strategy of your company. By monitoring financial perspectives, internal processes, customer perspectives, and learning and growth KPIs, you get a holistic view of performance. This approach can identify issues before they become problems and help you capitalize on your strengths.

Developing a dashboard that consolidates all these KPIs can greatly simplify the monitoring process. Use business intelligence (BI) tools to create real-time dashboards accessible from your devices. These dashboards can present data in easy-to-understand formats like charts and graphs, making it easier to interpret your business performance at a glance.

Establishing a periodic review cycle—be it monthly, quarterly, or annually—is crucial for evaluating KPIs consistently. These reviews provide an opportunity to reflect on past performance, set new targets, and adjust strategies as needed. They offer a structured way to assess the health of your business and ensure that you're on the path to long-term success.

By focusing on these Key Performance Indicators, you can steer your vending machine business towards sustained profitability and growth. Monitoring these metrics allows for data-driven decisions, fine-tuning operations, and ultimately making your vending machine endeavor not just a side hustle but a thriving business. Be diligent, adapt to what the numbers tell you, and continually strive for improvements. The rewards will manifest not just in revenue but in a well-oiled, profitable operation.

Conducting Regular Reviews

In the fast-paced world of vending machines, consistent performance evaluations are critical to maintaining profitability and ensuring long-term success. Simply setting up your machines and leaving them unattended is a recipe for disaster. Regular reviews allow you to stay on top of your business's health, identify any issues before they escalate, and capitalize on opportunities for improvement. It's akin to steering a ship; periodic checks ensure you stay on the right course.

To start, let's talk about the significance of performance metrics. When conducting regular reviews, you're essentially measuring your vending business's pulse. Whether it's monitoring sales, checking inventory levels, or assessing customer feedback, these reviews offer a treasure trove of data. Sales metrics reveal which locations are thriving and which need attention. Inventory metrics tell you what products are in high demand and which ones aren't moving. Customer feedback, often overlooked, provides insights directly from the people who keep your business afloat.

Utilizing data effectively requires a systematic approach. Begin with setting up a schedule for your reviews. Weekly reviews might focus on sales and inventory, while monthly reviews could dive into financial health and customer satisfaction. Quarterly reviews are ideal for comprehensive evaluations, including revisiting your goals and adjusting strategies as needed. Use software tools designed for vending machine management to track these metrics efficiently. A small investment in the right tools can yield substantial returns in the form of time saved and enhanced accuracy.

Now, you might be wondering, "What should I be looking for during these reviews?" Well, each review session should start by comparing collected data against predefined benchmarks. Are your sales figures meeting or exceeding expectations? Are your machines operating efficiently? Are there any recurring issues with product availability or functionality? A keen eye for detail will help you notice patterns, such as a consistently low-performing machine or a product that frequently sells out, indicating a need for reorder adjustments.

One critical aspect to scrutinize is machine maintenance, often overlooked until a problem arises. Routine checks ensure machines are in optimal working condition, minimizing downtime and maximizing revenue. Broken or malfunctioning machines not only lose money but also damage your reputation. Regular reviews allow you to stay proactive, scheduling maintenance before issues affect performance.

Additionally, take time to review your financial health. This isn't just about looking at your profits but understanding the underlying factors contributing to these financial results. Are your operating expenses creeping up? Are there inefficiencies in your supply chain that could be optimized? Regular financial reviews allow you to make data-driven decisions, adjust pricing strategies, and streamline operations to improve your bottom line.

Involving your team in these reviews can also be a game-changer. Scheduled team meetings to discuss review findings foster a culture of transparency and collective responsibility. Team members closest to daily operations may offer insights you hadn't considered, and brainstorming sessions can generate innovative solutions to encountered challenges. Collaborative reviews not only distribute the workload but also promote a sense of shared purpose and commitment to business success.

Another key benefit of regular reviews is the opportunity to pivot your marketing strategies. Examining which marketing efforts have yielded the best results over time can inform future campaigns. Have certain social media promotions boosted sales more than others? Has traditional advertising proven less effective? Adjust your marketing strategies based on these insights to ensure your promotional efforts align with actual performance data.

Customer feedback, another pivotal component of regular reviews, shouldn't be overlooked. Consumers are the lifeblood of your business, and understanding their needs and preferences is crucial. Use surveys, suggestion boxes, or digital feedback forms to collect this valuable data. Reviewing this feedback can highlight areas for improvement and potential new product offerings. Regularly integrating customer suggestions shows your audience that you value their opinions, fostering loyalty and repeat business.

Moreover, regular reviews pave the way for strategic growth. By setting short-term and long-term goals during these sessions, you can chart a clear path towards expansion. Whether it's adding more vending locations, diversifying your product range, or exploring innovative technologies, reviews help you stay focused and aligned with your business aspirations. They act as milestones along the journey, providing a clear sense of direction and achievement.

Let's not forget competition. Evaluating your competitors as part of your regular review can provide valuable insights and opportunities. What are they doing that you're not? Are there gaps in their service you could fill? Regularly benchmarking yourself against the competition ensures that you stay one step ahead, continually adapting to maintain your edge in the market.

Finally, documenting your review process and findings is vital. Keeping detailed records of what was discussed, the decisions made, and actions taken ensures continuity and accountability. It also allows you to track progress over time, providing a tangible sense of achievement as you see how far you've come. Future reviews can then benefit from this historical data, making each session more informed and efficient.

In summary, conducting regular reviews isn't just a good practice; it's an essential aspect of a successful vending machine business. By systematically checking your performance, engaging with your team, listening to your customers, and staying alert to the competition, you set the stage for continuous improvement and long-term success. It's your built-in mechanism for course corrections, growth, and sustainability. Commit to it, and your vending business won't just survive; it'll thrive.

Chapter 19: Case Studies of Success

In this chapter, we delve into compelling stories of vending entrepreneurs who turned their dreams into reality, showcasing the transformative power of a well-executed business strategy. You'll meet individuals like Sarah, who started with a single soda machine and grew her operation to over fifty units across several states, thanks to strategic location choices and relentless customer focus. Or take John, who leveraged modern payment systems and niche products to tap into underserved markets, achieving remarkable sales growth within his first year. These stories aren't just tales of financial success—they illustrate invaluable lessons in perseverance, creativity, and adapting to market changes. As you explore these case studies, you'll gain practical insights and inspiration to fuel your own vending machine venture, reminding you that with the right approach, the sky's the limit.

Interviews with Successful Vending Entrepreneurs

Navigating the world of vending machines involves more than just placing a few machines in strategic locations. Success requires a deep understanding of the business landscape, innovative strategies, and a keen eye for market trends. To illuminate these pathways, we've gathered insights from some of the industry's most thriving entrepreneurs. Their stories offer invaluable lessons and inspiration for anyone looking to break into the vending machine business.

One such entrepreneur is Jessica Taylor, who started her vending journey right out of college with a small loan and two second-hand machines. "I remember the excitement of setting up my first machines," she recalls. "It was a mix of fear and ambition. I spent countless nights researching the best locations and identifying my target audience." Jessica's strategy was simple but effective: she set up in busy office buildings where employees craved convenience. Her initial earnings might have been modest, but Jessica reinvested every dollar back into her business, gradually expanding her fleet. Today, she operates over a hundred machines across three states.

Beneath Jessica's success lies a foundational principle that many entrepreneurs echoed: the importance of location. Mark Wilson, another well-established vending operator, emphasizes this. "You can have the best products and top-of-the-line machines, but if they aren't in the right places, you won't see profits," he says. Mark's approach involved meticulous research. He spent weeks scoping out potential sites, analyzing foot traffic patterns, and even talking to locals to get a better sense of their needs. "It's about being in tune with your market," Mark asserts. "And sometimes that means adapting quickly to changing conditions."

Innovation also played a substantial role in the growth of these businesses. Brian Johnson, a tech-savvy entrepreneur, transformed traditional vending by incorporating technology. "I integrated cashless payment systems early on, back when it was still a novel concept," he shares. "It was a gamble, but it paid off. More people were willing to use my machines because they offered convenience." Brian didn't stop there. He embraced vending software that allowed him to track inventory in real-time, reducing manual labor and the risk of stockouts. By leveraging these tools, Brian scaled his operations efficiently and stayed ahead of his competitors.

Networking proved to be another cornerstone for these entrepreneurs. Take Susan Martinez, for example, who built her empire through strategic partnerships. "I attended every industry conference and workshop I could find," she says. "Those events were gold mines for networking." Susan made it a point to connect with property owners, fellow vendors, and suppliers. These relationships enabled her to secure coveted locations and access better deals on products. "Networking isn't just about exchanging business cards," she adds. "It's about forging relationships that can open doors you didn't even know existed."

Employee management is another critical aspect discussed by these entrepreneurs. Harold Green, who operates a large chain of vending machines in metropolitan areas, stresses the significance of having a reliable team. "You can't be everywhere at once," he states. "Hiring trustworthy employees who can manage day-to-day operations is essential." Harold implemented rigorous training programs and set clear guidelines to ensure consistency across his machines. His efforts paid off, allowing him to focus more on strategic growth rather than being bogged down with daily management issues.

Several entrepreneurs also pointed out the importance of customer feedback in shaping their businesses. Emily Carter, whose vending machines offer primarily healthy snack options, credits customer feedback for her niche's success. "I started with a mixed offering, but soon realized through customer surveys that there was a high demand for healthier options," she explains. Emily adapted her product mix accordingly, which not only satisfied her customers but also set her apart from competitors. "Listening to your customers isn't just about meeting their needs; it's about anticipating them," she emphasizes.

Risk management frequently surfaced in these conversations. Daniel Fox, a veteran in the vending industry with over two decades of experience, speaks candidly about the challenges he faced. "I've dealt with theft, machine failures, and even natural disasters," he recounts. Daniel's approach to managing these risks involved diversifying his portfolio and investing in high-security machines. He also established strong relationships with his suppliers, ensuring quick replacements for faulty machines. "Preparedness is key," he advises. "You should always have a contingency plan in place."

Lastly, many of these success stories highlight the emotional and psychological resilience required to thrive in this business. Jane Harper, who started with zero experience and now runs a flourishing vending enterprise, discusses the mental grit involved. "There were times I felt overwhelmed and considered quitting," she admits. "But I reminded myself why I started and stayed focused on my goals." Jane's perseverance paid off, and her story serves as a powerful reminder that setbacks are just stepping stones on the road to success.

In conclusion, the insights gleaned from these successful vending entrepreneurs underscore the multifaceted nature of the business. From meticulous location research and technological innovations to strategic networking and robust risk management, each element plays a crucial role. But perhaps the most significant takeaway is the blend of passion and persistence that drives success. Whether you're just starting out or looking to expand your existing operations, these narratives provide a wealth of knowledge and inspiration to guide your journey.

Lessons Learned

When diving into the world of vending machines, many entrepreneurs come with high hopes and varied expectations. Through the lens of successful individuals who have thrived in this field, a mosaic of lessons emerges that can serve both as cautionary tales and inspirational narratives. These lessons shaped their journeys, refined their strategies, and ultimately led to their success.

One essential lesson is the importance of adaptability. Markets change, consumer preferences evolve, and technological advances redefine how businesses operate. The stories of successful vending entrepreneurs stress the importance of staying nimble. For example, some entrepreneurs began with basic snack machines but diversified into healthier options as demand shifted. This adaptability enabled them to stay relevant and profitable despite changing market trends.

Another significant takeaway is the paramount importance of thorough market research. Successful vending machine operators meticulously analyze their target demographics and study consumer behavior. They identify what products sell best in particular locations and understand the competition's strengths and flaws. This insight often spells the difference between a thriving business and a failing one. Case studies reveal instances where initial ventures faltered due to inadequate research, only to rebound successfully once a strategic, informed approach was adopted.

The location of vending machines is another cornerstone of success. Several case studies highlight that prime locations make or break the business. Entrepreneurs who placed machines in high-traffic areas like malls, schools, and office buildings saw exponential growth compared to those who settled for less strategic spots. Negotiating beneficial agreements with property owners also emerged as a critical skill. Crafting mutually advantageous deals ensures both parties are happy, facilitating long-lasting partnerships.

Effective brand-building cannot be overstated. From designing eye-catching logos to crafting a memorable brand name, creating a strong brand identity is vital. Successful entrepreneurs often share that a strong brand not only attracts customers but also instills trust. This trust translates into repeat business and customer loyalty, both of which are essential for long-term success. Consistency in branding across all machines and marketing materials helps reinforce this identity, making the vending business stand out in a crowded marketplace.

Product sourcing stands out as another pivotal area. Many entrepreneurs learned the hard way about the value of reliable suppliers and the right product mix. Partnering with dependable suppliers ensures a steady stream of products, reducing instances of empty machines and unhappy customers. Furthermore, understanding which products appeal to the target demographic can boost sales. Experienced entrepreneurs often advise starting with a variety of products and then refining the selection based on sales data and customer feedback.

Pricing strategies significantly impact profitability. Case studies reveal that getting the price point right requires a delicate balance—too high, and you drive customers away; too low, and you undercut your profit margins. By analyzing competitor pricing and understanding market rates, successful entrepreneurs set prices that attract customers while still yielding a profit. Dynamic pricing strategies, such as adjusting prices based on time of day or location, have also proven effective.

Maintenance and technical know-how shouldn't be neglected. Frequent and proper maintenance keeps machines running smoothly, minimizing downtime and maximizing profitability. The case studies underline the importance of routine checks and prompt troubleshooting for common issues like coin jams or product misdispensations. Entrepreneurs have shared that a well-maintained machine not only operates efficiently but also speaks volumes about the business's reliability and professionalism.

Marketing, particularly leveraging social media and traditional methods, emerged as a vital tool for growth. Those who effectively utilized platforms like Instagram, Facebook, and Twitter to promote their vending machines saw increased engagement and sales. Traditional marketing methods, such as flyers and local ads, while often overlooked, also proved effective in specific contexts. Combining these approaches allows entrepreneurs to reach a wider audience and cultivate a robust customer base.

Legal considerations can't be overlooked. Licensing, permits, and zoning laws vary widely by location but ignoring them can result in hefty fines and disrupted operations. The value of consulting legal experts or leveraging local business development resources came up frequently in case studies. Entrepreneurs who took the time to understand and comply with all legal requirements laid a solid foundation for their ventures, avoiding potential pitfalls that could derail their business.

Financial management, including cash flow and accounting, is pivotal. Financial mismanagement can quickly lead to business failure. Successful entrepreneurs emphasize thorough bookkeeping and regular financial reviews. Keeping track of expenses, revenues, and profit margins helps in making informed decisions. Setting up automated accounting systems can simplify this process and reduce the risk of human error, enabling entrepreneurs to focus on strategic growth rather than daily financial management.

Innovations in technology and embracing automation have shown to be game-changers. Integrating cashless payment systems, for instance, caters to the growing number of consumers who prefer digital payments over cash. Additionally, using vending software for inventory management and sales tracking can significantly enhance operational efficiency. Entrepreneurs who embraced these technological advancements found themselves better equipped to meet customer expectations and manage their businesses more effectively.

While scaling a vending machine business, the significance of strategic planning and patience cannot be dismissed. Rapid expansion without adequate planning usually results in operational hiccups and financial strains. Case studies illustrate that growth is best achieved through gradual scaling, starting with a few machines, gaining experience, and then expanding based on robust strategies. Some entrepreneurs also explore franchising as a growth strategy, which, while promising, demands a solid infrastructure and clear operational guidelines.

Customer service holds a surprising amount of weight in the vending machine business. Promptly addressing customer complaints and maintaining strong customer relations can significantly impact a business's reputation. Happy customers are not only likely to return but also recommend your machines to others. Effective customer service includes easy-to-access contact information on machines and a proactive approach to solving any issues that arise.

Finally, it's crucial never to underestimate the importance of evaluating your success regularly. Key Performance Indicators (KPIs) provide a measurable way to assess how well the business is doing. KPIs like sales volume, machine uptime, and customer satisfaction are critical. Continuous reviews and refinements based on these metrics allow for targeted improvements and necessary pivots, ensuring sustained business growth.

In conclusion, success in the vending machine business is not a stroke of luck but the result of meticulous planning, continuous learning, and persistent effort. By understanding and applying the lessons learned from those who have already traversed this path, aspiring entrepreneurs can navigate the complexities and steer their ventures toward enduring success.

Chapter 20: Industry Trends and Future Outlook

The vending machine industry is constantly evolving, driven by both technological advancements and shifting consumer preferences. In recent years, we've seen a significant push towards healthier product offerings, with more machines dispensing snacks that align with dietary trends like organic, gluten-free, and vegan options. Cashless payment systems have also become a staple, accommodating the growing preference for digital transactions over traditional cash. Looking ahead, the integration of AI and the Internet of Things (IoT) will likely revolutionize inventory management and customer interaction, making machines smarter and more efficient. Entrepreneurs who stay ahead of these trends and adapt their business accordingly will find themselves well-positioned to capitalize on the opportunities that lie ahead, ensuring sustainability and growth in an increasingly competitive market.

Emerging Trends in Vending

As the vending machine industry evolves, staying ahead of emerging trends is pivotal for any entrepreneur looking to thrive. These trends not only shape the current landscape but also predict the future trajectory of the business. This section will delve into the latest innovations and shifts in consumer behavior that aspiring vending machine operators should be aware of.

One of the most significant trends we've seen is the rise of healthy vending. Consumers today are more health-conscious than ever, pushing demand for nutritious snack and drink options. Gone are the days when vending machines were only stocked with sugary drinks and salty snacks. From protein bars to organic fruit juices, the options are expanding, and many vending businesses are thriving by catering to this health-conscious market segment.

The trend towards healthy vending is complemented by the growing interest in plant-based and dietary-specific products. Gluten-free, vegan, and keto-friendly options are no longer niche; they are becoming mainstream. This shift requires vending machine operators to diversify their product offerings to meet these specific dietary needs. The ability to adapt and offer products that cater to diverse preferences can significantly boost sales and customer satisfaction.

Alongside the growing interest in health, another emerging trend is the adoption of cashless payment systems. With the world moving towards a cashless economy, vending machines equipped with card readers, mobile payment options, and even cryptocurrency compatibility are increasingly popular. Consumers appreciate the convenience, and operators benefit from quicker transactions and reduced theft. Integrating cashless systems also opens the door for more advanced technology, such as real-time inventory tracking and sales analytics.

Speaking of technology, smart vending machines are transforming the way the industry operates. These machines use IoT (Internet of Things) technology to provide real-time data on inventory levels, machine functionality, and consumer behavior. This data is invaluable for operators looking to optimize stock levels, preemptively address maintenance issues, and tailor their product offerings. The investment in smart technology often pays off through reduced operational costs and increased efficiency.

Another fascinating development is the rise of specialized vending machines. These machines go beyond snacks and drinks, offering a variety of products from electronics to personal care items and even gourmet meals. Airports, offices, and universities are prime locations for these niche machines. The diversification of vending machine products not only meets specific consumer needs but also allows operators to explore new market segments and revenue streams.

Alongside product diversification, the vending industry is witnessing an increase in customized and branded vending experiences. Companies are using vending machines as a marketing tool, customizing machines with their branding and offering promotional products. This strategy enhances brand visibility and engagement, turning a simple transaction into a memorable brand interaction. It's a trend that savvy operators can leverage by partnering with brands looking to increase their market presence.

Sustainability is also a key trend shaping the future of vending. Eco-friendly vending solutions, such as machines made from recycled materials and stocked with sustainable products, are gaining traction. Some operators are even implementing energy-efficient technologies and reducing plastic packaging to lessen their environmental impact. Consumers are increasingly making purchasing decisions based on a company's sustainability practices, so adopting green vending solutions can also attract eco-conscious customers.

Moreover, vending machine operators are exploring the concept of omnichannel retail. By integrating online and offline shopping experiences, operators can offer a seamless purchase experience. For instance, a consumer might order a product online and pick it up at a vending machine. This strategy bridges the gap between e-commerce and traditional retail, catering to the modern consumer's demand for convenience and speed.

Pop-up vending machines are another trend gaining momentum. These machines are used for limited-time offers, seasonal products, or specialty items. They create a sense of urgency and exclusivity, driving consumer interest and engagement. Pop-up vending also allows operators to test new products and concepts without committing to a permanent machine.

Lastly, the incorporation of artificial intelligence (AI) in vending machines is set to revolutionize the industry. AI can enhance user experience by providing personalized product recommendations based on past purchases. It can also optimize inventory management by learning consumption patterns and predicting demand more accurately. As AI technology continues to advance, its applications in the vending industry will likely expand, offering endless possibilities for innovation.

In conclusion, the vending machine business is at a fascinating crossroads, with numerous emerging trends that promise to reshape the industry. From health-conscious products and cashless payments to smart technology and sustainability, the opportunities for growth and innovation are vast. Aspiring entrepreneurs and current operators must stay informed and adaptable, leveraging these trends to build a thriving, future-proof business. Embracing these changes not only meets current consumer demands but also positions a vending business to lead in an increasingly competitive market.

Preparing for the Future

As we look ahead, the future of vending machine businesses presents a mix of exciting opportunities and unavoidable challenges. Navigating these elements successfully can define the ultimate success or failure of your entrepreneurial venture. Staying ahead of the curve requires foresight, adaptability, and an unwavering commitment to innovation.

The vending machine industry is evolving at a rapid pace, driven by advancements in technology, changing consumer preferences, and broader economic trends. For aspiring entrepreneurs and business owners, it's crucial to remain proactive and prepared for what's to come. Ignoring these shifts isn't an option if you aim to sustain and grow your business through the years.

Firstly, one cannot overstate the importance of keeping a finger on the pulse of technological advancements. From the incorporation of Internet of Things (IoT) capabilities to the rise of artificial intelligence, technology is revolutionizing how vending machines operate. Smart vending machines, equipped with sensors and connected to the internet, allow real-time monitoring of inventory, machine performance, and consumer purchasing behavior. This level of insight enables more efficient operations and can significantly boost profitability.

Implementing cashless payment systems is another trend that can no longer be ignored. Consumers are increasingly opting for digital payment methods, such as credit/debit cards, mobile wallets, and contactless payments. Integrating these systems into your vending machines is not just a convenience; it's becoming a necessity to stay competitive. Cashless payments can also reduce the risk of theft and lower the operational burden associated with handling cash.

Adapting to changing consumer preferences is equally important. Modern consumers are more health-conscious, environmentally aware, and value-driven than ever before. Stocking your vending machines with healthier options, eco-friendly products, and offering customizable choices are ways to cater to these evolving tastes. Leveraging data analytics to understand what your customers prefer will allow you to tailor your offerings effectively.

Another emerging trend is the integration of interactive features. Imagine a vending machine that not only dispenses products but also entertains or informs consumers through interactive screens, augmented reality (AR), or personalized recommendations based on purchase history. This not only creates a unique user experience but also fosters customer loyalty.

Sustainability is more than just a buzzword; it's a driving force behind many business decisions today. Eco-friendly practices such as using energy-efficient machines, biodegradable packaging, and reducing waste are not only good for the planet but also resonate well with consumers. The future will likely see stricter regulations in this area, so getting a head start now can serve you well in the long run.

Another area to keep an eye on is the economic environment. Fluctuating economic conditions can impact consumer spending power and business operations. For instance, during economic downturns, consumers may cut back on discretionary spending, which could affect vending machine sales. Having a diversified product range and being adaptable to price adjustments can help mitigate some of these challenges. The ability to pivot and adapt to new economic conditions will be essential.

Furthermore, understanding and anticipating changes in the legal landscape is crucial. Regulations surrounding vending machines, such as health and safety standards, data privacy laws, and payment system compliances, are continually evolving. Staying informed and ensuring compliance with these regulations will prevent legal troubles down the line.

Networking and professional development will play a significant role in preparing for the future. Joining industry associations, attending relevant conferences, and participating in workshops will keep you updated on the latest trends and innovations. They also provide valuable opportunities for networking, allowing you to form partnerships and collaborations that can be beneficial for your business.

Finally, consider the scalability of your business. As trends and technologies evolve, your ability to scale efficiently will determine your long-term success. This might involve diversifying your machine locations, exploring franchising opportunities, or expanding product lines. Staying agile and prepared to seize new opportunities as they arise will keep your business ahead of the competition.

In conclusion, preparing for the future in the vending machine industry isn't just about responding to immediate challenges; it's about anticipating what's next and positioning your business to take advantage of emerging opportunities. Whether it's through technological advancements, adapting to consumer preferences, or maintaining sustainability, being prepared means being proactive. The future belongs to those who are ready to embrace change and leverage it for growth.

Chapter 21: Dealing with Competition

In the rapidly evolving vending machine business, competition is inevitable and addressing it effectively can make all the difference between success and stagnation. One of the keys to thriving in a competitive landscape is to adopt a competitive pricing strategy that ensures your offerings remain attractive without sacrificing profit margins. Equally important is differentiation—standing out in the crowded market through unique product selections, superior customer service, and eye-catching branding. Building strong relationships with vending location owners and continuously optimizing your machine placements for maximum visibility can also set you apart. Ultimately, maintaining a keen awareness of your competitors' actions while focusing on delivering consistent value to your customers will empower you to stay ahead. Innovation and adaptability will be your best allies in this competitive journey.

Competitive Pricing Strategies

When you're running a vending machine business, competitive pricing strategies are the lifeblood of your operation. Setting the right prices isn't just about covering costs and making a profit; it's about striking a delicate balance between offering value to your customers and undercutting your competition. The goal is to ensure that customers see your machines as the best option while allowing you to maintain healthy profit margins.

To start, it's crucial to conduct thorough market research. Study your competitors' pricing and analyze the trends in the areas where your vending machines are located. Are there any seasonal price variations? Are certain items priced higher in some locations than others? By understanding the pricing landscape, you can tailor your strategy to fit both local and broader market conditions. Competitive intelligence can give you insights into how others in the industry are positioning themselves, helping you make informed decisions.

An essential part of competitive pricing is knowing your costs inside and out. Direct costs such as product procurement, transportation, and machine maintenance should be meticulously calculated. Don't forget indirect costs like utilities, rent (if you're paying for premium locations), and even the cost of financing. Only by understanding your complete cost structure can you set prices that are both competitive and profitable. It's a juggling act, but one that pays off in the long run.

Sometimes, strategic underpricing can be your friend. Launching a new vending machine with a 'market penetration pricing' strategy can help attract customers quickly. By setting lower prices temporarily, you can lure customers away from competitors and build your customer base. Once you've established a solid reputation and loyal customer base, you can gradually raise the prices without losing business. Remember, volume often compensates for lower margins. The more products you sell, even at a slightly reduced price, the more revenue you'll generate.

On the flip side, premium pricing can also work wonders. If your vending machines offer specialized, high-quality, or hard-to-find items, don't be afraid to price them accordingly. Customers are often willing to pay a little extra for convenience, quality, or niche products they can't find elsewhere. Positioning your brand as a premium option can differentiate you from budget competitors and attract a different segment of customers willing to spend more.

Dynamic pricing is another innovative strategy. With the help of technology, you can adjust prices in real time based on various factors such as demand, time of day, and even weather conditions. For example, you might notice a surge in demand for cold drinks during hot weather. Raising prices slightly during these peak times can boost your revenue without alienating customers. Conversely, during low-demand periods, offering discounts can attract more sales and keep your products moving.

The art of bundling shouldn't be overlooked either. Creating value packs or bundling slower-moving items with popular products can increase overall sales. For example, if you have a snack that's flying off the shelves but a beverage that's lagging, consider offering a combo deal. This not only helps clear out old stock but also provides perceived value to the customer, making them feel like they're getting a good deal.

Promotional pricing can be highly effective as well. Limited-time offers, discounts for bulk purchases, or loyalty programs can incentivize customers to choose your vending machines over competitors'. These tactics can create urgency and repeated business, further cementing your machines as go-to sources for convenient, affordable snacks and drinks. Promotions don't always have to erode your margins; think of them as investments in customer acquisition and retention.

Price matching can also be an effective yet competitive strategy. If competitors in your area offer a lower price for the same product, consider matching or even slightly undercutting their prices. Customers appreciate the effort and are more likely to stay loyal to your brand if they know you offer the best deals. However, use this tactic sparingly to ensure it doesn't eat into your profits too significantly.

Another advanced strategy involves segmenting your markets. Pricing can be adjusted based on different demographics, locations, and even vending machine types. For instance, a vending machine located in a high-end gym can have different pricing compared to one situated in a public park. Understanding your market segments can help you tailor your pricing strategies to fit the unique needs and behaviors of different customer groups.

Even psychological pricing plays a role. Small differences, like setting a price at $1.99 instead of $2.00, can significantly impact a customer's perception of value. This tiny adjustment can make customers feel like they're getting a better deal, even though the difference is negligible. Implementing these subtleties across your product range can cumulatively improve your profitability.

Of course, competitive pricing strategies should never be static. Regularly revisit and revise your pricing models. Keep an eye on competitors, market trends, and your own sales data. Use this information to iteratively refine your approach. Successful vending machine operators often conduct quarterly reviews or even more frequent assessments to ensure their pricing remains competitive and in line with their overall business goals.

It's also vital to have some flexibility in your pricing to adapt to unexpected changes, like new competitors entering the market or sudden shifts in consumer behavior. A dynamic, responsive pricing strategy will help you stay ahead of the curve, ensuring your vending machines remain the preferred choice for customers.

Ultimately, competitive pricing strategies are not about having the lowest prices across the board. They're about smart, strategic pricing that takes into account your costs, market conditions, and customer value perception. By continually refining and adapting your pricing strategies, you'll not only outshine your competition but also build a thriving, profitable vending machine business that's sustainable in the long run.

Differentiation Tactics

When it comes to running a vending machine business, the competition is fierce. Differentiation tactics are crucial to setting yourself apart in a crowded market, where other entrepreneurs are also vying for the same prime locations and customer base. The essence of differentiation is simple: make your vending business stand out in ways that are valuable to your customers. Let's explore several methods that will help you carve a unique niche for your vending machine business.

First, consider the products you offer. If every vending machine on the block is stocked with the same sodas and snacks, why would anyone go out of their way to use yours? This is where you can let your creativity shine. Think about offering unique, healthier options such as organic snacks, vegan treats, or locally-sourced products. These niche items may command a higher price, but they also attract a loyal customer base that values quality over affordability.

Another excellent way to differentiate is through the appearance and branding of your vending machines. Bland, generic machines blend into the background, but vibrant, creatively branded machines draw attention. A well-designed logo and eye-catching graphics can significantly impact customer perception. Additionally, having your machines well-lit and clean says a lot about your business's commitment to quality and customer satisfaction. Effective branding can be a game changer, making your machines a preferred choice in high-traffic areas.

Location can also serve as a powerful differentiator. While it's great to land spots in shopping malls or office parks, think outside the box. Consider locations like gyms, schools, or even co-working spaces where the offerings can be tailored to the specific audience. For example, energy bars and protein shakes are perfect for gym-goers, whereas stationery and light snacks might be more appropriate for educational institutions. By customizing your stock to the needs of the location, you not only offer convenience but also relevance, making your machines indispensable.

Customer engagement is another vital piece of the differentiation puzzle. Utilizing advanced vending technology, like touch screens and interactive displays, can captivate your audience. Consider integrating social media features where customers can instantly share their purchases or experiences, thereby spreading the word about your business. Another idea is to implement loyalty programs, where frequent users can accumulate points or receive discounts. These small touches can make a big difference in customer retention.

Speaking of technology, embracing other tech advancements can give you an edge over your competitors. Cashless payment systems, for instance, offer both convenience and security. Digital wallets, NFC payments, and mobile apps broaden your customer base by making it easier for people to make purchases. Moreover, using vending software to monitor stock levels and machine health in real time can lead to more efficient operations and quicker response times, ensuring your machines are always in optimal condition.

Strategic partnerships can also help set your business apart. Collaborate with local businesses, gyms, or schools to create mutually beneficial relationships. For instance, a gym could offer memberships or special discounts through your vending machine, while you provide them with a share of the profits. Such partnerships can enhance your credibility and broaden your customer base, giving you a solid advantage over the competition.

Another tactic is to offer a variety of sizes and pricing tiers for products. People appreciate having choices, and by offering smaller, budget-friendly options alongside premium products, you cater to a broader audience. This approach can attract both cost-conscious customers and those willing to splurge on something special.

Let's not forget the power of data. Collecting and analyzing data on customer preferences and purchasing behavior can provide invaluable insights. For example, you might discover that certain products perform better at specific locations or times of the year. Utilizing this data to refine your product offerings and restocking schedules can dramatically enhance customer satisfaction and increase sales.

Ethical practices can also serve as a distinguishing factor. Today's consumers are increasingly concerned about sustainability and corporate responsibility. Incorporating eco-friendly packaging or ensuring that your suppliers adhere to ethical guidelines can win the loyalty of socially conscious customers. Promoting these practices through your branding and marketing materials can draw attention to the positive impact of doing business with you.

Lastly, consider the versatility of your vending machines. Beyond food and beverages, many unconventional items can be sold through vending machines – think tech gadgets, beauty products, or even art supplies. By diversifying your offerings, you can tap into markets that are often overlooked by traditional vending businesses, thus broadening your scope and enhancing your uniqueness.

In conclusion, successful differentiation in the vending machine business hinges on a combination of superior product offerings, strategic locations, savvy use of technology, and strong customer engagement. It's about understanding your customers' needs and exceeding their expectations in ways that your competitors do not. By innovating and continuously adapting, you can carve out a distinctive, profitable niche in the vending machine market.

Chapter 22: Managing Risks and Challenges

Every entrepreneurial venture comes with its share of risks and challenges, and a vending machine business is no different. Recognizing potential pitfalls early on can save you time, money, and a lot of stress down the road. From vandalism to machine malfunctions, you'll find that anticipating issues before they arise is key. Insuring your machines and products can offer a safety net in case of unexpected events. Diversifying your product range and staying informed about market trends can mitigate demand risks and keep your business resilient. Equally important, establishing solid relationships with reliable suppliers ensures you won't face product shortages. By employing these strategies, you'll stand better equipped to navigate the complexities of managing your profitable vending machine business smoothly and efficiently.

Identifying Potential Risks

Embarking on a vending machine business, like any venture, is fraught with potential risks. To navigate these treacherous waters successfully, you need to be aware of the various hazards that could disrupt your operations and profitability. Knowing what to look out for is the first step in mitigating these risks.

First and foremost, location is a critical factor. If your machines are not placed in optimal spots, you won't see the traffic needed to make your business profitable. High-traffic areas like malls, schools, and offices are ideal, but even within these locations, placement matters. A vending machine tucked away in a corner might not perform as well as one situated near an entrance or gathering area. Conduct thorough market research to determine the best possible locales for your machines.

An often-overlooked risk is machine maintenance. Vending machines are mechanical devices, and like any machine, they can break down. Routine maintenance is essential to ensure they function smoothly. A single malfunctioning machine can result in lost sales and customer dissatisfaction. It's also important to understand the common problems that vending machines encounter, such as jammed coin mechanisms or product dispensers, and have quick solutions at hand.

Theft and vandalism are another major risk. Vending machines are public-facing, making them susceptible to tampering. Investing in machines with robust security features can deter potential thieves. Additionally, placing your machines in monitored, secure areas can help mitigate this risk. Surveillance cameras and regular inspections can act as further deterrents.

Product spoilage is a significant concern, especially if you're dealing with perishable items like snacks or beverages. Maintaining an optimal inventory level is crucial to avoid overstocking, which can lead to expired products. Conversely, understocking can leave customers frustrated when they don't find the items they want, driving them to competitors. Utilizing inventory management software can help keep track of stock levels and identify high-turnover products that need frequent replenishment.

Supplier reliability can make or break your business. Dependable suppliers ensure that you get quality products on time. A disruption in the supply chain can lead to empty machines and lost revenue. Establish relationships with multiple suppliers to have backup options if one vendor fails to deliver for some reason. Don't put all your eggs in one basket; diversification can provide an added layer of security.

Legal and compliance issues also pose significant risks. Failure to adhere to local regulations regarding vending machine placement, health standards, and business licensing can result in fines or operational shutdowns. Ensure you are up-to-date with all local laws and regulations and maintain thorough records. It's wise to consult with a legal professional specializing in vending laws to ensure full compliance.

Technological advancements, while offering numerous benefits, can also pose risks. For instance, the integration of cashless payment systems can attract tech-savvy customers but can also make your machines vulnerable to cyber-attacks. Employ robust cybersecurity measures to protect customer data and ensure the security of transactions.

Economic fluctuations are external risks that can impact your vending business. Changes in the economy can affect consumer spending patterns. During economic downturns, people may cut back on discretionary spending, including vending machine purchases. Staying informed about economic trends and being prepared to adjust your business strategies accordingly can help cushion these effects.

The competitive landscape can also pose significant risks. New entrants into the vending machine market can disrupt your revenue streams. It's crucial to stay ahead by continually analyzing your competitors and differentiating your offerings. Whether it's through unique product selections, superior customer service, or innovative machines, maintaining a competitive edge is essential.

Seasonality is another factor to consider. Depending on the locations of your vending machines, sales may fluctuate with the seasons. For example, vending machines in school locations might see a dip in sales during the summer months when schools are closed. Being aware of these patterns can help you plan your inventory and staffing needs accordingly.

Lastly, don't underestimate the impact of customer preferences and behavior changes. As consumer tastes evolve, a product that was once a bestseller might fall out of favor. Continually gather customer feedback and stay attuned to market trends to adapt your product offerings. This adaptability can help you stay relevant and maintain customer satisfaction.

Identifying potential risks in your vending machine business is not just about recognizing what could go wrong; it's about preparing for these eventualities. Comprehensive risk management involves not only planning for known risks but also being agile enough to respond to unforeseen challenges. By taking the time to identify and understand the risks associated with your business, you're better equipped to develop strategies that will help you mitigate these risks and keep your vending machine business on the path to success.

Mitigation Strategies

In the vending machine business, as with any entrepreneurial endeavor, risks and challenges are a given. But rather than being deterred by these potential pitfalls, it's essential to embrace them with a proactive mindset. Effectively managing risks can be the difference between a successful operation and a business that struggles to break even. This section will guide you through comprehensive mitigation strategies to help safeguard your vending machine venture.

One of the primary strategies for risk mitigation is diversifying your machine locations. By spreading your machines across various high-traffic areas, you reduce the dependency on a single site for your revenue. This means if one location underperforms, the impact on your overall business will be minimized. Consider installing machines in office buildings, malls, and schools to reach different demographics. Each venue brings its own set of patrons, thus broadening your customer base.

Maintenance of vending machines is another critical area to focus on. Downtime due to machine malfunctions translates directly to lost revenue and dissatisfied customers. Implementing a rigorous routine maintenance schedule ensures your machines stay in top shape. Regular inspections for wear and tear, prompt repairs, and software updates can prevent minor issues from becoming major headaches. Investing in reliable, high-quality machines at the beginning can also reduce the frequency and cost of future maintenance.

Insurance is a tool often overlooked by budding entrepreneurs, but it's crucial for managing risks effectively. Comprehensive coverage can shield your business from a range of unforeseen events, such as theft, vandalism, or natural disasters. Additionally, liability insurance protects you if a customer is injured while using your machine. Consult with an insurance agent to tailor a plan that meets the specific needs of your vending machine business.

Choosing the right suppliers is fundamental in mitigating product-related risks. Reliable suppliers ensure that your machines are consistently stocked with quality items. Establishing long-term relationships and negotiating written agreements can lock in favorable terms and prices, reducing the risk of supply chain disruptions. Always have backup suppliers to avoid sudden shortages, which could lead to empty machines and lost customers.

Data analytics can be a powerful ally in risk management. By frequently analyzing sales data, you can identify trends and predict customer preferences, thus allowing you to adjust your product offerings proactively. Data-driven decision-making helps optimize inventory, reducing both overstocking and stockouts. Familiarize yourself with vending software that can assist in tracking sales, inventory levels, and even machine maintenance schedules.

Pricing strategy plays a crucial role in risk mitigation, too. While it's tempting to undercut competitors on price, this can erode your profit margins. Instead, focus on providing value. Higher-priced, premium products can often yield better margins and attract a more loyal customer base. Combine this with occasional discounts or loyalty programs to keep your customers engaged and satisfied.

Legal considerations must never be overlooked. Ensuring compliance with all relevant laws and regulations minimizes the risk of fines and legal action. From obtaining the necessary licenses and permits to adhering to zoning laws, every detail matters. Keep abreast of changing regulations in your area and consult with a legal advisor if you're unsure of specific requirements. Being proactive in this regard can save you costly headaches down the line.

A solid financial management strategy is essential for mitigating economic risks. This includes everything from setting up a robust accounting system to managing cash flow effectively. Regular financial reviews can help you spot discrepancies early and take corrective action. Diversifying your income streams within the vending business—such as adding new types of machines or offering advertising space on your machines—can provide added financial security.

Security investment is another aspect not to be overlooked. Modern vending machines should be equipped with security features such as surveillance cameras, tamper-proof locks, and cashless payment systems. These measures can deter theft and vandalism, reducing the associated costs and inconvenience. Partner with reputable security firms to ensure that these systems are consistently updated and maintained.

Customer service excellence can also act as a buffer against risks. Happy customers are less likely to lodge complaints and more likely to return. Implement a system for prompt response to customer feedback, whether it's through a dedicated phone line, email, or social media channels. Transparency and active engagement can turn a potentially negative situation into an opportunity for strengthening your brand loyalty.

Finally, staying informed about industry trends and innovations can give you a competitive edge. Attend trade shows, join industry associations, and participate in workshops to stay ahead of the curve. Understanding emerging trends—like the shift towards healthy snacks or the use of eco-friendly products—allows you to adapt before these become mainstream, positioning your business as a leader rather than a follower.

By employing these mitigation strategies, you're not just avoiding potential pitfalls; you're building a resilient business model capable of weathering the storm and emerging stronger. Risks will always be present, but with preparation and adaptability, you can navigate challenges successfully and create a thriving vending machine business. The key is to remain vigilant, proactive, and always open to learning and improvement.

Chapter 23: Sustainability and Eco-Friendly Practices

In today's world, integrating sustainability and eco-friendly practices into your vending machine business isn't just a nice-to-have—it's essential. Not only do green practices help the environment, but they also resonate with increasingly conscious consumers who are willing to support businesses that share their values. Start by choosing energy-efficient vending machines that minimize power consumption and operate seamlessly. Consider sourcing products that use minimal packaging or opting for suppliers with robust recycling programs. Additionally, implementing a regular maintenance schedule ensures your machines run efficiently, reducing waste and extending their lifespan. By embracing these eco-friendly strategies, you're not only reducing your carbon footprint, but also creating a competitive edge that can attract a loyal customer base, ultimately driving profitability and long-term success.

Green Vending Solutions

In today's world, sustainability isn't just a buzzword; it's a necessity. For those venturing into the vending machine business, embracing eco-friendly practices can set you apart from the competition and appeal to a growing market of conscious consumers. Going green with your vending solutions not only helps the environment but also enhances your brand's reputation, leading to increased customer loyalty and potentially higher profits.

One of the first steps in implementing green vending solutions is choosing energy-efficient vending machines. Look for machines with Energy Star certifications, which signify that they meet strict energy efficiency guidelines set by the Environmental Protection Agency (EPA). These machines consume less energy, reduce operational costs, and have a lower environmental impact. By opting for energy-efficient options, you're not only saving money in the long run but also positioning your business as a forward-thinking, responsible entity.

Next, consider the products you stock. Select eco-friendly, locally sourced, and ethically produced items whenever possible. Organic snacks, beverages with minimal packaging, and products from companies that practice sustainable manufacturing can all contribute to a greener vending operation. By offering these choices, you appeal to health-conscious and environmentally aware consumers, who are often willing to pay a premium for products that align with their values.

Reducing waste is another crucial aspect of green vending solutions. Implement systems to recycle and properly dispose of waste generated from your vending operations. Many vending machines can now be equipped with recycling compartments for bottles and cans, encouraging customers to recycle on the spot. Additionally, you can use biodegradable or recyclable packaging for products, further minimizing the environmental footprint of your business.

Incorporating renewable energy sources is another game-changer. Solar-powered vending machines, for instance, are increasingly available on the market. These machines harness solar energy to operate, significantly cutting down on electricity usage from non-renewable sources. While the initial investment might be higher, the long-term savings and environmental benefits make it a worthwhile consideration.

Let's not forget about transportation. The logistics of restocking machines can contribute significantly to your carbon footprint. Opt for fuel-efficient vehicles or explore electric vans for your inventory transportation needs. Planning efficient routes and schedules can also minimize fuel consumption and reduce emissions. In doing so, you're not just cutting down on costs, but also showing a commitment to eco-friendly practices.

Smart technology and automation also play a vital role in green vending solutions. Advanced telemetry systems can help you monitor your vending machines remotely, optimizing restocking schedules and ensuring machines are always running efficiently. These technologies can alert you to potential issues before they become problems, reducing waste and downtime. Automated inventory management helps minimize excess stock and ensures products are sold before their expiration dates, further reducing waste.

Employee training in sustainability practices is equally important. Ensure your team is well-versed in the green objectives of your business. Simple actions, like turning off lights when machines are not in use or ensuring proper disposal of waste, can significantly impact your sustainability goals. Employees who understand and embrace eco-friendly practices can become ambassadors for your brand, promoting green values and enhancing customer relations.

Partnerships can also bolster your sustainability efforts. Collaborate with suppliers who are committed to sustainable practices and can provide eco-friendly products. Establishing relationships with organizations that focus on environmental conservation can lead to joint initiatives that benefit both parties. Whether it's a local farm supplying organic produce or a recycling company helping manage waste, these partnerships can enhance your credibility and impact.

Publicizing your green efforts is key. Market your eco-friendly initiatives through various channels—social media, your website, and even on the vending machines themselves. Transparency about your sustainability practices can build trust and attract a loyal customer base that values environmental responsibility. Highlight milestones, such as energy savings achieved or waste reduced, to show tangible results of your green initiatives.

Lastly, stay informed about emerging sustainability trends in the vending industry. Innovations are constantly evolving, and staying ahead of the curve can give your business a competitive edge. Attend industry conferences, read up on the latest research, and actively seek out new technologies and practices that can further enhance your green vending solutions. A commitment to continuous improvement in sustainability not only benefits the environment but also positions your business as a leader in the field.

Investing in green vending solutions is more than just a trend; it's a strategic move that can have long-term benefits for your business, your customers, and the planet. By embracing energy-efficient machines, eco-friendly products, waste reduction, renewable energy, and smart technology, you can create a vending machine business that's sustainable and profitable. So, take the leap towards green solutions—because the future of vending is undoubtedly green.

Benefits of Sustainability

In today's business landscape, embracing sustainability isn't just a trend; it's a strategic move that translates to tangible benefits for your vending machine business. Whether you're an aspiring entrepreneur or a seasoned business owner, integrating eco-friendly practices into your operations can enhance profitability and reputation. So let's delve into why sustainability is not just a buzzword but a cornerstone for a thriving business.

Firstly, sustainable practices can significantly reduce operational costs. Utilizing energy-efficient vending machines, for instance, can lower electricity bills. Modern vending machines equipped with LED lighting and efficient cooling systems consume less power, translating to substantial savings over time. Moreover, machines with sleep mode options can further cut down energy consumption during off-peak hours. These savings, though they might seem incremental, can add up and provide a healthy boost to your bottom line.

Aside from cost savings, sustainability attracts a growing segment of eco-conscious consumers. Public awareness about environmental issues is at an all-time high, and more people prefer to spend their money with businesses committed to eco-friendly practices. By branding your vending machines as "green" or "eco-friendly", you appeal to this demographic, potentially increasing sales. Think about prominently displaying sustainability badges or certifications on your machines or through marketing campaigns. This not only elevates your brand's image but also builds a loyal customer base that values your commitment to the environment.

On top of consumer preference, your commitment to sustainability can open up new markets. In certain jurisdictions, local governments or organizations prioritize businesses that demonstrate eco-friendly operations. Incorporating sustainable practices might make you eligible for grants, subsidies, or tax incentives provided by government programs aimed at promoting green business practices. These financial aids can further reduce your costs and support business expansion efforts.

Additionally, adopting sustainable practices can bolster employee satisfaction and motivation. Employees today, particularly younger generations, are increasingly looking for workplaces that align with their values. By championing sustainability, you create a positive workplace culture that can attract top talent. Employees who believe in the company's mission are usually more engaged and productive. They take pride in working for a company that's making a difference, and this morale boost can translate to better service and operations.

Let's not forget the positive impact on community relations. Sustainability initiatives often involve engaging with the local community, which can foster goodwill and improve your business's standing. For instance, you could participate in local recycling programs or community clean-up events. These activities not only preserve the environment but also enhance your business's image as a responsible community member. Clients and customers are more likely to support businesses that actively contribute to the well-being of their local area.

Furthermore, sustainable practices help mitigate risks associated with environmental regulations. Governments worldwide are tightening regulations surrounding waste management, emissions, and energy consumption. By staying ahead of the curve and adopting best practices early, your business can avoid potential fines and legal issues. Compliance with environmental regulations not only safeguards your business but also ensures long-term operational stability.

Then there's the aspect of differentiation. In a competitive market, setting your vending machine business apart can be challenging. Sustainability offers a unique selling proposition (USP) that differentiates you from competitors who might not prioritize eco-friendly practices. This distinction can be particularly advantageous in saturated markets where consumers have multiple options. Emphasizing your green initiatives can make your business the preferred choice when customers weigh their options.

Moreover, the shift towards sustainability is closely linked with innovation. Embracing eco-friendly solutions often involves adopting new technologies or innovative business models. For example, the use of IoT (Internet of Things) technology can optimize energy use and improve the efficiency of your vending machines. Such innovations can not only reduce your environmental footprint but also streamline operations, making your business more agile and responsive to market demands.

It's also worth noting the long-term viability that comes with sustainability. Businesses that integrate sustainable practices are generally more resilient. They are better equipped to navigate challenges such as resource scarcity or fluctuating energy prices. By relying on renewable energy sources or sustainable materials, you can stabilize your supply chains and ensure uninterrupted operations. In the long run, this resilience can be a critical factor in the longevity and success of your business.

Finally, there's an intrinsic satisfaction that comes from running a sustainable business. Knowing that your operations minimize harm to the environment and contribute to a better future can be incredibly fulfilling. This sense of purpose can drive you and your team to continually improve and innovate. It's not just about financial gain; it's about making a positive impact that transcends the business itself.

In summary, the benefits of sustainability in your vending machine business are multifaceted. From cost reductions and customer loyalty to regulatory compliance and market differentiation, the advantages are clear. Sustainability isn't merely an ethical choice; it's a strategic one that can propel your business towards long-term success and stability. By embedding eco-friendly practices into every facet of your operations, you don't just build a profitable business—you contribute to a healthier, more sustainable world.

Chapter 24:0
Networking and Professional Development

Building a profitable vending machine business goes beyond securing prime locations and having the right machines and products—it's about forging essential connections in the industry. Networking and professional development play crucial roles in this journey. By joining industry associations, attending conferences, and participating in workshops, you'll enhance your knowledge, stay abreast of emerging trends, and learn best practices from seasoned professionals. These opportunities not only provide valuable insights but also open doors to potential partnerships and mentorships. Engaging with peers in the industry through these channels can lead to collaborative ventures, shared resources, and support systems that are vital for long-term success. Remember, the relationships you build can propel your business forward by fostering innovation, resilience, and growth.

Joining Industry Associations

When you're venturing into the vending machine business, one of the best steps you can take for your professional growth is joining industry associations. These associations serve as hubs for networking, gaining industry insights, and staying ahead of emerging trends. It's not just about shaking hands and exchanging business cards—it's about accessing a treasure trove of resources that can give your business a competitive edge.

Firstly, let's consider the practical benefits. By becoming a member of a vending machine association, you often gain access to members-only resources such as research reports, market data, and tools that would otherwise be very costly or difficult to obtain. This data can help you make informed decisions about your business, whether you're choosing new machine locations, negotiating with suppliers, or setting prices. In turn, this could directly impact your revenue and growth.

Another major advantage is the opportunity for continuous learning. Many associations offer webinars, training sessions, and certification programs that are designed to keep you updated with the latest advancements and best practices in the vending industry. In an ever-evolving sector, staying educated is crucial for maintaining a competitive edge. Plus, this continuous learning can be an excellent source of motivation and inspiration for both you and your team.

Networking is one of the cornerstones of joining industry associations. Attending association meetings, mixers, and other networking events can open doors to new opportunities and partnerships. Imagine being able to brainstorm ideas with other seasoned vending machine business owners or learning from their experiences and mistakes. You might even find a mentor who can provide guidance and insight as you navigate the challenges of growing your business.

Additionally, being part of an association can significantly boost your credibility in the eyes of potential clients, partners, and customers. Membership often signals that you are committed to upholding industry standards and staying informed about the latest trends and practices. This can be a strong selling point when negotiating contracts or trying to expand into new locations.

Industry associations also offer advocacy. They often have a collective voice and lobbying power that can be used to influence legislation and regulations that affect the vending machine industry. This can be particularly beneficial if new laws or modifications to existing laws are being proposed that could impact your business. Knowing there's a group of knowledgeable professionals advocating for your interests can provide some peace of mind.

Being part of an industry association can also expose you to innovations and new technologies that can make your vending machine business more efficient and profitable. For instance, associations frequently host trade shows where suppliers and tech companies showcase their latest products. From the newest cashless payment systems to eco-friendly vending solutions, you get to see—and often try out—the latest advancements before they become mainstream.

Moreover, associations usually have newsletters or magazines that keep you informed about the latest news, trends, and best practices in the vending machine business. These publications can be an excellent resource for articles on improving operational efficiency, new marketing strategies, and even case studies of successful vending businesses. Consistently reading these materials can keep you inspired and informed.

Lastly, don't underestimate the emotional and psychological benefits of being part of a professional community. Running a vending machine business can sometimes feel isolating, especially if you're mainly interacting with machines and locations rather than people. Being part of an industry association provides a sense of belonging and the support that comes from knowing others are facing similar challenges and working towards the same goals.

While there are dues and fees associated with joining most industry associations, many members find that the benefits far outweigh the costs. Think of your membership as an investment in your professional development and your business's future. The resources, knowledge, and connections you gain can be invaluable assets as you work to build a profitable and sustainable vending machine business.

Attending Conferences and Workshops

Conferences and workshops present an invaluable opportunity to deepen your understanding of the vending machine industry and build essential connections. Embracing the mind-set of a lifelong learner broadens your vision, equipping you with up-to-date knowledge and trends that could just set you apart from the competition. From keynote speeches to interactive sessions, these events are a cocktail of inspiration and practical learning.

The essence of attending these gatherings extends beyond mere education. You're positioning yourself in an arena filled with like-minded individuals, all driven by a common goal of achieving excellence in the vending business. Here, you'll find a mix of fellow entrepreneurs, industry veterans, suppliers, and even potential partners or investors. Each individual carries with them a unique perspective and experience.

Let's not overlook the practical insights you can gain from workshops. These focused sessions often tackle specific aspects of the vending machine business, such as advanced troubleshooting techniques, innovative product sourcing strategies, or cutting-edge technology integrations. Remember, knowledge is power, and the more you accumulate, the stronger your business foundation becomes.

Imagine attending a workshop where experts break down the nuances of vending software or the latest cashless payment systems. This firsthand exposure can help you leapfrog common hurdles and implement more efficient, profitable systems in your own operations. Plus, being part of interactive sessions where you can ask questions and receive immediate answers is invaluable.

The networking aspect of conferences cannot be emphasized enough. During breaks, at lunch, or even in casual conversations, you can exchange contact details with people who could become future mentors, collaborators, or friends. Building these relationships can open doors to new opportunities, whether it's finding a prime location, gaining access to exclusive products, or even discovering a groundbreaking marketing tactic.

Another dimension to consider is the motivation and inspiration that such events radiate. Listening to success stories and overcoming challenges often injects a renewed sense of purpose and energy into your entrepreneurial journey. It's a reminder that every leader, no matter how successful, started from scratch and faced their own set of obstacles.

Let us not forget the access to industry-specific resources. Many conferences feature expos where vendors showcase their latest products, machines, and technology. This is your chance to see, touch, and even test new innovations before they hit the mainstream market. It's a way to stay ahead of the curve and ensure that your vending business remains competitive and cutting-edge.

Workshops often provide you with takeaway materials—booklets, handouts, even digital resources that you can refer to long after the session has ended. These materials can serve as a valuable reference, helping you to implement and maintain best practices in your business operations over the long haul.

Moreover, these events offer an excellent platform for you to share your own experiences and insights. Speaking at a conference or leading a workshop not only positions you as a thought leader but also allows you to give back to the community. It's an opportunity to inspire and help others who are on the same journey that you've embarked upon.

Another significant advantage of these events is that you can often earn continuing education credits. These credits not only add value to your professional credentials but also keep you up-to-date with industry standards and practices. Many associations and professional groups recognize these credits, making it easier for you to maintain certifications or memberships.

Attending conferences and workshops can also help you stay compliant with legal and industry standards. Often, sessions cover the latest regulations and compliance issues, ensuring that you avoid unexpected fines and penalties. Staying informed about these changes protects your business and helps you operate ethically and legally.

For those new to the industry, these events can serve as a crash course. The information density at these gatherings is unmatched, providing you with a wealth of knowledge in a short period. It's an efficient way to get up to speed and become familiar with best practices and industry norms.

Don't underestimate the value of the social aspect of these events either. Informal gatherings, such as dinner parties or mixers, provide a relaxed environment to build deeper connections. These personal relationships often translate into business opportunities down the line, whether through partnerships, collaborations, or simply by having someone to bounce ideas off.

Furthermore, many conferences offer post-event engagements, like online communities or follow-up webinars. These platforms allow you to continue learning and engaging with industry leaders and peers long after the event has ended. It's an ongoing resource that keeps you in the loop, informed, and inspired.

The importance of attending conferences and workshops in your journey as a vending entrepreneur cannot be overstated. They offer multifaceted benefits, from practical knowledge and resource acquisition to networking and inspiration. Make it a point to attend these events regularly, and you'll find that they play a crucial role in the growth and success of your vending machine business.

Chapter 25: Exit Strategies and Succession Planning

Planning your exit from the vending machine business isn't just about packing up and moving on; it's a strategic process that ensures the legacy and profitability of your hard work continue. Whether you're considering selling your business to a third party, transitioning it to a family member, or even merging with another enterprise, having a detailed succession plan is crucial. Start by thoroughly evaluating your business's worth, analyzing financial statements, and understanding market conditions. It's essential to create a timeline for your exit, outlining key milestones and deadlines. Additionally, you'll want to communicate your plans clearly with stakeholders and prepare any potential successors with the knowledge and skills they need to succeed. A well-thought-out exit strategy not only maximizes your profits but also ensures that your vending empire continues to thrive under new leadership.

Planning Your Exit

Planning an exit strategy is a vital, yet often overlooked, component of building a successful vending machine business. It's easy to get caught up in the day-to-day operations and growth strategies, but knowing when and how to step away is just as important. Start thinking about your exit plan early on, regardless of how far you are into your business journey. Whether you aim to sell your business, pass it on to a family member, or simply retire, planning your exit should align with your overall business goals and personal aspirations.

One of the first steps in crafting an exit strategy is to envision your future and what you want it to look like. Where do you see yourself in five, ten, or twenty years? If your goal is to retire, at what age do you plan to do so? Do you want to remain involved in the business in some capacity, or are you looking for a clean break? Answering these questions will help shape your exit strategy and determine the timeline and steps needed to achieve it.

Documentation is another crucial aspect of planning your exit. Keep thorough and updated records of all business transactions, contracts, and agreements. These documents will not only keep your business running smoothly but will also be critical when the time comes to exit. Potential buyers or successors will want to review comprehensive and well-organized records to understand the business' financial health and operational intricacies.

Valuation of your vending business is another critical element. Understanding the current market value of your business helps in setting a realistic price when you're ready to sell. Regular valuations will provide insights into factors that can increase or decrease your business's value. Focus on increasing revenue streams, reducing operational costs, and maintaining the physical condition of your vending machines to add value to your business.

Succession planning is equally important, especially if you intend to pass the business down to a family member or a trusted employee. Identify and groom a potential successor early in your business journey. This process involves training them in every aspect of the business, from daily operations to long-term strategic planning. An effective succession plan ensures continuity and stability, maintaining the trust of both customers and suppliers.

Involving legal advisors and accountants in your exit planning can make the process smoother and more efficient. These professionals can guide you through the complexities of selling a business, including tax implications, legal requirements, and financial documentation. Their expertise can help you avoid costly mistakes and ensure that you get the best possible return on your investment.

One effective strategy is setting specific milestones or benchmarks as part of your exit plan. These milestones could include reaching a certain profit level, having a defined number of vending machines in operation, or securing a stable customer base. Achieving these benchmarks signals that your business is in a strong position, making it more attractive to potential buyers.

If selling your business is part of your exit strategy, marketing it effectively is crucial. Just as you market your vending machines to customers, you'll need to market your business to potential buyers. Highlight the strengths of your business, such as high traffic locations, reliable supply chains, and strong customer relationships. Providing detailed financial reports and growth projections can also bolster buyer confidence.

Consider potential buyers carefully. Someone with experience in the vending machine industry or a similar field may be more likely to understand the day-to-day operations and challenges. This kind of buyer is also more likely to value your business appropriately and see its potential. However, don't discount interested parties from different backgrounds—they may bring fresh perspectives and innovative ideas to the table.

Your employees are an essential part of your exit strategy. Their morale and productivity can significantly impact your business's value. Keep them informed about your plans and involve them in the transition process where appropriate. If your employees are happy and well-informed, they're more likely to stay with the business, providing stability for the new owner.

Flexibility is another key aspect of a successful exit strategy. The business environment is always changing, and your exit plan should be adaptable to these changes. Regularly review and revise your strategy to reflect current market trends, economic conditions, and personal circumstances. Being flexible ensures that your exit plan remains relevant and effective, regardless of when you decide to implement it.

Finally, consider the emotional aspect of exiting your business. Many entrepreneurs find it challenging to let go of something they've built from the ground up. It's essential to prepare yourself emotionally and mentally for this transition. Surround yourself with a support network of family, friends, and business advisors who can provide guidance and encouragement during this significant change.

In summary, planning your exit is a multifaceted process that requires careful thought and strategic planning. By starting early, keeping detailed records, valuing your business accurately, grooming a successor, involving professionals, setting milestones, marketing effectively, considering potential buyers, maintaining employee morale, being flexible, and preparing emotionally, you can ensure a smooth and successful transition. As a vending machine business owner, having a well-structured exit plan not only protects your investment but also sets the stage for the future, whether it's for retirement, a new venture, or the next chapter in your life.

Selling Your Business

At some point, every business owner will face the decision of whether to sell their business. In the vending machine industry, selling your business can be both a strategic exit plan and a lucrative opportunity. Before embarking on this journey, there are essential steps and considerations to ensure you maximize the value and appeal of your business to potential buyers.

First, let's evaluate why you might want to sell your vending business. Personal reasons often drive this decision, including retirement, a shift in career interest, or a desire to cash in on the business's success. Sometimes, the market itself may dictate the decision; perhaps it's at an all-time high, and you want to capitalize on favorable conditions. No matter your reasons, preparing your business for sale requires both financial and operational mindfulness.

Before you list your vending business for sale, it's crucial to have a thorough professional valuation conducted. This not only gives you a realistic idea of what your business is worth but also provides potential buyers with the confidence that they're making a wise investment. Valuation factors typically include earnings, growth potential, the stability of your existing locations, and the overall state of your machines and equipment.

Next, you should get your financials in impeccable order. Transparent, well-documented financial records are non-negotiable for serious buyers. Ensure you have detailed income statements, balance sheets, and cash flow statements readily available. These documents should ideally cover at least the past three years to show consistent performance and growth. It's also crucial to highlight any long-term contracts with suppliers or property owners for your vending machine locations, as these can add significant value.

Aside from financial documentation, you'll want to present the operational strengths of your business. This includes outlining your established routes, vending machine conditions, types of products sold, and relations with suppliers and service contractors. Buyers will be keen to understand if they are stepping into a well-oiled machine or if there's substantial work to be done. Demonstrating streamlined operations and efficiency can make your business far more attractive.

Additionally, don't underestimate the importance of having a robust customer service strategy in place. When selling a vending machine business, the buying decision could hinge on customer loyalty and satisfaction. Showcase your approach to handling customer complaints and maintaining positive relations. Highlighting strong customer service records can significantly boost your business's perceived value.

The process of finding buyers can vary, but there are several effective avenues to explore. Listing your business on various online marketplaces specifically for business sales, such as BizBuySell or BusinessBroker.net, can be an excellent starting point. Networking within industry associations and attending relevant conferences can also yield potential buyers who are already familiar with the vending market and its dynamics.

Finding the right broker can be a game-changer. A professional with experience in the vending industry knows the ins and outs and can help negotiate better deals. Their knowledge and networks can lead to faster sales and higher selling prices. However, thoroughly vet potential brokers by checking references and past successes.

Another crucial step is preparing a sale memorandum or a pitch document. This document should provide an overview of your business, including financial summaries, operational details, market position, and growth opportunities. Essentially, it's your business's resume, crafted to make it as appealing as possible to potential buyers.

Legal considerations can't be overlooked. Selling a business involves creating and reviewing substantial legal paperwork. Having an attorney who specializes in business sales can ensure you're adequately protected and that all legal documentation is comprehensive and compliant.

Once you have potential buyers, it's essential to conduct thorough due diligence. Just as buyers will scrutinize your business, you should scrutinize buyers to ensure they have the financial capability and intent to follow through with the purchase. Vetting a potential buyer properly can save you from future headaches.

Negotiations can be the most delicate part of the process. Be prepared to discuss price, payment terms, and transitional periods. Often, new owners will request a transition period where you might stay on temporarily to assist with training and operations handover. Being flexible and open in these negotiations can facilitate a smoother sale.

Closing the deal involves finalizing the sale agreement, transferring ownership, and situating new management, if applicable. This step also requires precise coordination with legal representatives, accountants, and brokers to ensure everything is in order.

Post-sale, reflect on the entire journey and what you've accomplished. Selling a business is not just the end of an era; it's a transition that can open new opportunities for you. Whether it's venturing into a new industry, taking time off, or investing in new projects, the sale of your vending machine business can be the stepping stone to your next adventure.

Ultimately, selling your business is a multifaceted process that requires careful planning, a clear strategy, and an understanding of the market. By diligently preparing your vending machine business for sale, you'll position yourself to achieve a successful and profitable exit, allowing you to reap the rewards of your hard work and dedication.

Conclusion

Your journey into the world of vending machines is now fully equipped with a treasure trove of information, insights, and actionable strategies. As we wrap up this comprehensive guide, let's focus on the big picture and the essential takeaways that will drive your success.

First and foremost, the vending machine business is an incredible opportunity for aspiring entrepreneurs. It's an industry that operates on convenience—something society values more than ever. The blend of passive income potential with the flexibility to scale according to your ambitions makes it a lucrative endeavor. Remember, the foundation of any successful business is a clear and achievable goal. Without setting specific and measurable objectives, you're essentially navigating without a map. Refer back to Chapter 2 when you need to refine or reassess your goals.

Now, from setting goals to choosing the right locations, each step in the process of establishing your vending machine business is interconnected. The decisions you make in selecting prime spots (Chapter 4) will directly influence your market penetration and, consequently, your profitability. It requires you to be shrewd, leveraging both high-traffic areas and well-negotiated agreements with property owners.

Beyond physical locations, understanding your market and your competition (Chapter 5) is key. Identifying your target demographics and knowing what your competitors offer will help you carve out your niche. This knowledge will also influence your choices in product sourcing (Chapter 7) and pricing strategies (Chapter 8). Remember, your market's preferences should drive your product mix and price points. Always be willing to adapt based on customer feedback and sales data.

Branding is another pillar of your venture (Chapter 6). A memorable brand name and visually appealing logo will set you apart from generic vending machines and contribute immensely to customer loyalty. In today's digital age, don't underestimate the power of online presence combined with traditional marketing methods (Chapter 10). Consistent messaging across all channels will reinforce your brand identity.

Maintenance and troubleshooting are where the rubber meets the road (Chapter 9). Downtime can be costly, so routine maintenance is not just advisable—it's imperative. Regular checks and being prepared for common issues will save you time and money, keeping your machines operational and customers happy.

Financial management will ensure the long-term viability of your business (Chapter 12). From setting up robust accounting systems to managing cash flow, the financial health of your business is crucial. Don't overlook the importance of technology either (Chapter 15). Integrating cashless payment systems and utilizing vending software can streamline operations and enhance customer experience.

Automation tools can lighten your workload significantly (Chapter 16). Whether it's automating inventory management or transaction records, these innovations can free up your time to focus on scaling your business (Chapter 17). And when it comes to scaling, the sky's the limit. Explore new markets, consider franchising, and always keep an eye on your KPIs (Chapter 18).

Real-world examples from Chapter 19 show that success in the vending machine business is more than theoretical; it's entirely achievable. Learning from those who've walked the path before you provides valuable lessons and keeps you grounded.

As you navigate issues of competition (Chapter 21) and manage risks (Chapter 22), always consider sustainability (Chapter 23). Eco-friendly practices are not just good for the planet—they're often good for business too. Modern customers appreciate green solutions, and these can become a key differentiator for your brand.

Networking and ongoing professional development (Chapter 24) shouldn't be overlooked either. Join industry associations, attend workshops, and keep your finger on the pulse of evolving trends (Chapter 20). Being an active member of the business community can open doors and provide support that's indispensable.

Finally, always plan for the future, including your potential exit strategy (Chapter 25). Someday, you might want to sell your business or pass it on. Preparing for that moment well in advance can maximize the value and ensure a smoother transition.

The appendix offers sample business plans, useful templates, and a host of additional resources that will serve you well as references. Don't hesitate to revisit these materials. The knowledge shared here is a starting point; your operational experience will add depth and nuance over time.

In conclusion, venturing into the vending machine business is not just about filling machines with products. It's about fulfilling customer needs, making strategic decisions, and continually evolving. Armed with the insights and strategies from this book, you're now ready to build a profitable and sustainable business. May your vending machines stand as symbols of convenience and quality, reflecting the passion and precision you've invested. Here's to your success!

Appendix A: Appendix

This appendix serves as a valuable resource hub to complement the main content of this book. It's designed to arm you with practical tools and further reading that will aid your journey in starting, managing, and scaling a profitable vending machine business. Below are sections that you can refer to whenever you need additional support or templates for your business operations.

Sample Business Plans

Creating a solid business plan is crucial to the success of your vending machine business. This section includes sample business plans that you can customize according to your specific needs and goals. By reviewing these samples, you'll get a better idea of how to structure your plan, outline your objectives, and detail your strategies for reaching them. Remember, a well-crafted business plan is your roadmap to achieving success.

Useful Templates and Checklists

Whether you're just starting out or are already managing several machines, keeping organized is key. Here, you'll find a variety of templates and checklists that will help streamline your operations. These include:

- Startup Checklists: Essential steps to take before launching your business.

- Monthly Maintenance Templates: Keep track of routine maintenance tasks to ensure your machines run smoothly.

- Inventory Management Sheets: Stay on top of stock levels and plan restocking efficiently.

- Financial Tracking Tools: Easily monitor your cash flow, expenses, and revenue.

- Marketing Campaign Planners: Organize your marketing strategies and track their effectiveness.

- Customer Feedback Forms: Gather valuable insights from your customers to improve your service.

Further Reading and Resources

Knowledge is power, and the journey to a successful vending machine business doesn't end with this book. This section offers a curated list of further readings and resources to deepen your understanding and inspire continued growth. These resources include:

- ***Books:*** Advanced texts on entrepreneurship, marketing strategies, and business management.

- ***Websites:*** Trusted industry blogs and websites that provide the latest news and trends in vending.

- ***Online Courses:*** Educational platforms offering courses on business development and automation tools.

- ***Networking Groups:*** Forums and social media groups where you can connect with other vending machine business owners and share insights.

By leveraging the tools and resources provided in this appendix, you'll be well-equipped to tackle the challenges of your vending machine business head-on, ensuring sustained growth and profitability.

Sample Business Plans

Creating a business plan is one of the most important steps in launching a vending machine business. It's not just a document to show potential investors but also a blueprint for your operations, strategies, and financial projections. This section contains a few sample business plans that will guide you in crafting your own.

Let's start with a basic vending machine business plan. This plan is centered around a simple yet effective concept: providing easily accessible snacks and beverages within a corporate office environment.

For instance, imagine a setting where office employees are often too busy to step out for a quick snack. Here, vending machines can save the day. The focus should be on high-demand products such as coffee, bottled water, energy drinks, and healthy snacks. Identify a couple of high-traffic office buildings as your initial locations.

A comprehensive business plan for this scenario would include:

- **Executive Summary:** Outline your business goals, the services you're offering, and a brief overview of your target market.

- **Business Description:** Detail what type of vending machines you will be using, and explain why you chose the specific office buildings as your target locations.

- **Market Research:** Include data on the demand for vending services in corporate environments, focusing on employee behavior and preferences.

- **Marketing Strategy:** Discuss how you plan to reach out to property managers or business owners to secure your locations.

- **Operational Plan:** Outline the logistics of stocking and maintenance, specifying your scheduling, suppliers, and any storage facilities for bulk items.

- **Financial Plan:** Provide revenue projections, estimate the initial working capital, and outline a break-even analysis.

Next, let's consider a specialized vending machine business focusing on healthy, organic products in gyms and fitness centers, tapping into the growing health-conscious market. This approach needs a slightly different plan because the product mix and target demographic vary significantly.

For this scenario, a solid business plan might include:

- **Executive Summary:** Describe the mission to provide convenient, healthy snack options to gym-goers and fitness enthusiasts.

- **Business Description:** Explain the unique advantage of offering a product line focused on organic, non-GMO, and gluten-free snacks and beverages.

- **Market Research:** Provide insights into the fitness market, including statistics on the growing trend of health and wellness.

- **Marketing Strategy:** Show how you plan to collaborate with gym owners, use social media, and possibly leverage influencer partnerships.

- **Operational Plan:** Highlight the logistics of sourcing high-quality products, maintaining freshness, and coordinating restocking schedules.

- **Financial Projections:** Expect higher product costs due to quality specifications but balance this with premium pricing, forecasting revenue and expenses.

Considering a vending machine business in hospitals and healthcare settings requires a tailored plan as well. Here, the focus shifts to providing quick, nourishing, and easy-to-consume items for busy healthcare professionals and patients' families.

Elements of this business plan might include:

- **Executive Summary:** Explain your goal to support hospital staff and visitors with convenient, nutritious meal and snack options.
- **Business Description:** Highlight the strategic placement within hospital cafeterias, waiting areas, and break rooms.
- **Market Research:** Include statistics on hospital foot traffic and common dietary preferences within healthcare environments.
- **Marketing Strategy:** Describe how you will secure facility approvals and possibly partner with hospital administrations.
- **Operational Plan:** Address stocking needs, particularly considering dietary restrictions common in hospitals, and plan for frequent maintenance.
- **Financial Plan:** Detailed projections, combining the cost of specialized products with the potential for regular, high-volume sales.

In each of these scenarios, it's crucial to keep in mind that no business plan is set in stone. Adapt and revise based on feedback, financial performance, and market trends. Successful entrepreneurs are flexible, continually refining their approach as they gather more data and experience.

Finally, consider a business model focusing on automated retail kiosks in airports. This takes the vending concept to another level with a wider range of products including electronics, travel accessories, and gourmet snacks.

Your business plan for airport kiosks should encompass:

- **Executive Summary:** Emphasize your aim to cater to travelers with convenient and essential items available on the go.

- **Business Description:** Discuss the types of products to be offered and the configurations of the automated kiosks.

- **Market Research:** Provide data on airport foot traffic, traveler demographics, and spend patterns.

- **Marketing Strategy:** Highlight strategies for securing prime spots within airports, possibly through revenue-sharing agreements with airport authorities.

- **Operational Plan:** Explain how you will manage inventory, incorporate security measures, and ensure the reliability of the machines.

- **Financial Projections:** Focus on the high potential for impulse purchases and high margins on travel-essential products.

Remember, these sample plans are jumping-off points. The specifics of your business plan will depend heavily on your unique vision, resources, and market conditions. Tailor each aspect of the plan to reflect your business's strengths and opportunities, and don't hesitate to seek professional advice for fine-tuning.

In conclusion, a well-thought-out business plan is not just a formal document—it's a reflection of your business aspirations and strategic outlook. Armed with the right plan, you'll be well-positioned to navigate the complexities of the vending machine industry and capitalize on the lucrative opportunities it offers.

Useful Templates and Checklists

As you embark on your vending machine business journey, having a set of prepared templates and checklists can be incredibly valuable. These tools will not only save you time but also ensure that you cover all your bases efficiently. This section is designed to provide you with practical templates and checklists that align with each stage of your business development, from inception to daily operations. Let's dive into the assortment of templates and checklists you'll find useful along the way.

First and foremost, every vending machine business should start with a solid *business plan template*. This template usually includes sections for your executive summary, market analysis, business structure, product line, marketing strategies, and financial projections. A comprehensive business plan can serve as your roadmap, guiding you through the critical steps required to get your business off the ground.

When you're ready to launch, consider using a **site assessment checklist**. This will help ensure you choose the best locations for your vending machines. Key elements of this checklist might include foot traffic analysis, demographic fit, proximity of competing machines, and potential bargaining points for lease agreements. Ensuring your locations are prime can significantly impact your revenue potential.

As you build your brand, a well-organized *branding checklist* is essential. This should cover everything from securing a memorable domain name to designing consistent branding materials. Whether it's logo creation, color schemes, or taglines, staying consistent across all platforms helps build brand recognition and trust among customers.

Next, you'll need a **supplier vetting template**. This ensures that you are sourcing products from reliable and cost-effective suppliers. The template should include criteria like supplier reputation, product quality, pricing, delivery timelines, and payment terms. Knowing you're stocking your machines with quality items is crucial for customer satisfaction and repeat business.

Once your vending machines are up and running, regular maintenance and troubleshooting become critical. A *machine maintenance checklist* can be a lifesaver. This list should detail routine checks such as replenishing stock, cleaning the machine, inspecting for wear and tear, and software updates. Regular maintenance helps reduce downtime and increases machine longevity.

A **troubleshooting log template** can also be beneficial. Documenting common problems and their solutions allows you to resolve issues more quickly. The log should include problem identification, steps taken to resolve it, and any follow-up actions required. This documentation often becomes invaluable, saving you both time and frustration.

Effective inventory management is another critical aspect of your business. Implementing an *inventory tracking sheet* will help you keep tabs on stock levels and identify best-selling items. This sheet can be as simple as an Excel spreadsheet or a more sophisticated software system, depending on your needs and budget. Regularly updating your inventory helps optimize your product mix and prevent stockouts.

Cash flow management is often cited as one of the most challenging aspects of running a small business. A **cash flow statement template** can simplify this process. It typically includes sections for income, expenses, and net cash flow, tracked on a monthly basis. Keeping a close eye on your cash flow ensures you meet all financial obligations and can reinvest in growing your business.

Customer satisfaction is the lifeblood of your vending machine business. A *customer feedback form template* can provide invaluable insights into what you're doing right and areas for improvement. Whether you use physical feedback forms attached to your machines or digital surveys accessible via QR codes, gathering and responding to customer feedback can drive improvements and loyalty.

For legal compliance and due diligence, a **licensing and permits checklist** is essential. This list helps you track all required local, state, and federal permits and licenses needed to operate your machines legally. Missing even one required permit could lead to hefty fines or shutdowns, making this checklist a critical element of your business operations.

For marketing purposes, a well-designed *marketing campaign checklist* can streamline your promotional activities. This checklist might include steps for social media posts, email newsletters, promotional events, and advertising tactics. Keeping your marketing efforts organized ensures you're consistently and effectively reaching your target audience.

As your business scales, you may find the need for a **hiring checklist**. This will guide you through the process of recruiting and onboarding new team members. Elements of this checklist might include job descriptions, interview questions, reference checks, and initial training programs. Onboarding the right people smoothly and efficiently can be a significant asset to your growing business.

During your business operations, a *daily operations checklist* can help ensure that you and your team stay on top of essential tasks. This should include daily cash collection schedules, restocking routines, and customer interaction protocols. A thorough operations checklist makes sure nothing falls through the cracks and keeps your business running smoothly day in and day out.

Expanding your business might lead you to consider franchise opportunities. A **franchise evaluation template** can be invaluable for this. It should cover aspects like market potential, initial investment, support from the franchisor, and potential ROI. Evaluating these factors comprehensively can help you make an educated decision on whether franchising is the right path for your business expansion.

Lastly, you'll want a *regular review and performance tracker* to evaluate your success. This might include monthly and quarterly reviews of key performance indicators (KPIs) such as sales volume, machine uptime, customer satisfaction scores, and more. Regular reviews help you identify trends and make data-driven decisions to steer your business toward greater success.

In conclusion, these templates and checklists serve as practical tools to organize and streamline your vending machine business operations. By leveraging these resources, you'll be better equipped to handle the various aspects of your business, from start-up to expansion. Remember, the preparation and organization you do today will pay dividends tomorrow. Stay focused, stay organized, and watch your vending machine business flourish.

Further Reading and Resources

Building a successful vending machine business demands an ongoing commitment to learning and growth. For entrepreneurs wanting to dive deeper, explore beyond this book by tapping into a wealth of knowledge and resources. Start by identifying reliable books, journals, and online publications that focus on various aspects of the vending machine industry. One recommended read is "Secrets of the Vending Machine Business" which delves into the nuances of running a profitable vending machine endeavor.

Next, consider subscribing to industry-specific magazines such as "Vending Times" and "Automatic Merchandiser." These publications can keep you updated about the latest trends, success stories, and technological innovations within the vending world. Furthermore, these sources often feature in-depth articles on diverse subjects—from detailed market analyses to informative pieces on cutting-edge products and services.

For a more practical learning experience, you can turn to webinars and online courses offered by experts in the field. Web platforms like Coursera and Udemy frequently offer courses in small business management, marketing, and financial planning—skills indispensable to running a vending machine business. Make sure to look for courses tailored specifically for vending operators to gain actionable insights and practical knowledge.

Networking also plays a critical role in expanding your business acumen. Joining professional associations like the National Automatic Merchandising Association (NAMA) can provide countless benefits. Membership often includes access to industry reports, mentoring opportunities, and exclusive events where you can network with others in the field. Being part of such groups can give you insights that are just not accessible elsewhere.

For those tech-savvy entrepreneurs, numerous apps and online tools exist to streamline business operations. Inventory tracking systems, route planning software, and financial management tools can all make a big difference. Software like VendSoft and Seed Pro help you manage and track your vending operations more efficiently, giving you more time to focus on scaling your business. These tools often provide free trials, so you can experiment before committing financially.

Audio resources such as podcasts also offer a valuable way to consume industry knowledge without compromising on time. Shows like "Vending Machine Business Start-Up Podcast" offer practical advice, interviews with successful operators, and tips for improving your business. Listening to these podcasts can be incredibly motivational and can also offer real-world advice from people who have been in your shoes.

Professional mentorship can be invaluable when you're charting your path in the vending machine industry. Organizations such as SCORE connect small business owners with seasoned mentors who can offer advice on everything from business planning to daily operations. Don't underestimate the value of having a mentor who can provide direct, personalized advice based on extensive industry experience.

Attending industry trade shows and conferences can open doors that would otherwise remain closed. Events like The NAMA Show draw vendors, suppliers, and entrepreneurs together, offering opportunities to build relationships that can prove invaluable in the long run. At these events, you can see the latest in vending technology, discuss solutions with suppliers, and gain insights from keynote speakers renowned in the industry.

Additionally, leveraging online forums and discussion groups can be a great way to connect with peers. Websites like Reddit and industry-specific forums provide platforms where you can ask questions, share insights, and learn from the experiences of other vending machine operators. These communities often address common challenges and solutions, further enriching your knowledge base.

While it's crucial to stay knowledgeable about the basics, diving into complementary business areas can also be advantageous. Reading about consumer behavior, sales psychology, and emerging technology trends can furnish you with comprehensive knowledge to stay ahead. Books like "Influence: The Psychology of Persuasion" can provide insights that help tailor your product selection and marketing strategies.

Financial planning and management are the backbones of any successful vending business. Books such as "Profit First: Transform Your Business from a Cash-Eating Monster to a Money-Making Machine" offer great advice on managing business finances effectively. These teachings can be instrumental in ensuring your vending business remains profitable and sustainable over the long haul.

Finally, never underestimate the power of online business communities. Websites like LinkedIn feature professional groups where industry leaders and new entrepreneurs discuss the latest market trends, share case studies, and provide support. Joining these groups can provide ongoing learning and networking opportunities crucial for long-term success.

To sum up, the journey to building a profitable vending machine business doesn't stop once you've set up your initial operations. Continually seeking out further reading and resources ensures you stay ahead of the curve, adapt to industry changes, and seize opportunities when they arise. Stay curious, stay connected, and never stop learning.

www.ingramcontent.com/pod-product-compliance
Lightning Source LLC
Chambersburg PA
CBHW030005190526
45157CB00014B/440